THE COURAGE

Finding the ability to conquer your fears
and align with God's plan for your life

31-Day Prayer Journal

Kendria McKnight
MAKE FEAR HOMELESS CHRISTIAN PUBLISHING COMPANY
COVER PHOTO TAKEN BY DERRICK BOYKINS

Scriptures taken from the Holy Bible, New International Reader's Version®, NIV® Copyright © 1995, 1996, 1998, 2014 by Biblica, Inc.® Used by permission of Zondervan. www.zondervan.com The "NIrV" and "New International Reader's Version" are trademarks registered in the United States Patent and Trademark Office by Biblica, Inc.®

Scripture taken from the Amplified Bible, Copyright © 1954, 1958, 1962, 1964, 1965, 1987 by The Lockman Foundation. Used by permission.

The Courage to Fish, 31-Day Prayer Journal—*Finding the ability to conquer your fears and align with God's plan for your life*

Copyright © 2021 by Make Fear Homeless Christian Publishing Company

All rights reserved. Published and printed in the United States of America. No part of this book may be reproduced or transmitted in any form or by any means without written permission from the author.

Published by: Make Fear Homeless Christian Publishing Company

Email: info@makefearhomeless.com

Website: www.makefearhomeless.com

I dedicate this prayer journal to:

God: Who loved and created me with vision and purpose. I thank you for entrusting me with spiritual gifts that give you glory.

My husband, Juan Sr.: I love you, bae. Thank you for loving me for over 31 years. I appreciate your support of whatever God is asking me to do. I love that after all of these years together, you still make me laugh. Thank you for listening to me, even when I talk during your football game. I love that you laugh at my jokes, even though I often mess up the punchlines. And thank you for bringing me into your world of fishing. Thank you for teaching me how to fish.

My children, LaShonna, Teota, Juan Jr., and Ashayla: I love you all so much. I am happy that God gave you all to me. Thank you for loving me, unconditionally. I don't always get the "mom thing" right, but you don't give up on me. You remain in my daily prayers. God gave each of you unique gifts, and even if you were not my children, I would want all of you in my life.

My mom: Thank you so much for your love, prayers, and support in everything I do. You always have a word of encouragement, and I appreciate that so sincerely. Thank you for never forgetting to celebrate my birthday. You are my rock.

My brothers, Ed, Kevin, and Terry: I love you all. Thank you for loving me, protecting me, teaching me life skills, good and bad. Our father passed when I was very young, and all of you stepped in to fill the void. I am who I am because of all of you. You each have an extraordinary place in my heart.

My sister and best friend, Tanya: I love you so much. I thank God that we are sisters and best friends. You are one with whom I can share my dreams, visions, and fears, and you never judge me or laugh. You always encourage me to be what God has called me to be. You see in me what I often can't see in myself. You speak life to me always. Although I am older, your voice comforts me. I love the way you give advice and walk by my side every step of the way. I will love you forever.

My friend Sheya: Words cannot express how much I love you. I appreciate your wisdom, words of encouragement, and patience with me. Thank you for not getting frustrated when I kept making excuses for not completing this journal. You have walked with me through the most challenging times of my life. Thank you.

Pastor and First Lady Toliver and the entire Progressive Church of God in Christ family: I love you all. Thank you for all of your unconditional love and support of me.

Contents

Introduction 7
Day 1 Getting to the Root 9
Day 2 Picture Perfect 13
Day 3 It's Just Not Enough 15
Day 4 Just Follow 17
Day 5 Stay on That Wall 20
Day 6 Roll Away the Stone 22
Day 7 Trusting Evidence 25
Day 8 My Wake 27
Day 9 It Seems Impossible 29
Day 10 Know the Way 32
Day 11 This Seems Weird 35
Day 12 Not Like the Rest 38
Day 13 I Am Trying 41
Day 14 Hear His Voice 44
Day 15 It's Complicated 47
Day 16 Superb Workmanship 50
Day 17 Trust the Process 52
Day 18 Resist the Urge to Continue 55
Day 19 Take It to Jesus 57

Day 20 Take a Rest 59

Day 21 The One 61

Day 22 Say What? 64

Day 23 What Do You Know? 67

Day 24 Knowing the Difference 69

Day 25 Going With the Flow 71

Day 26 Following Directions 74

Day 27 Overcoming Fear 77

Day 28 Time With Jesus 80

Day 29 Not What I Expected 83

Day 30 Seeing the Light 87

Day 31 He Sees Me 90

Introduction

Without hesitation, I can say that 2010 and 2011 were the most challenging years of my life. After praying for God's will for my life, I hit my bottom. This challenge would require me to dig deep into my soul and identify what was in my heart. What I believed about Jesus and his power in my life was now in question.

I had a choice to make. Would I fight my way out of this trial and lean to my own understanding? Or would I rest in the love that I knew Jesus has for me? Resting in the love of Jesus required me to believe that Jesus is exactly who the Bible says he is. All my years of Bible study, prayers, and worship were in question. This is where the rubber meets the road.

After struggling daily for an entire year, things were not getting better. Then, one day, while sitting in my car for my daily cry, the Lord met me there. He reminded me of his love for me and that I was going to survive. He was going to fight for me. This day, things begin to turn in my favor. I think my life turned because I began to believe Jesus.

After a few months, I decided to go with my husband to an annual fishing tournament. Let me help put this in perspective and mention that I don't know how to swim. And I didn't know much about fishing because that was my husband's hobby. I don't think it is just a hobby for him; he loves to fish. This opportunity was a "win-win" because I wanted to get away from my current issues, and he needed a fishing partner.

We purchased a used boat off Craigslist, and I bought a very cute pink and white fishing pole for the tournament. Since I am a bit of a diva, I wanted my fishing gear to be color-coordinated for the event.

I quickly learned that fishing was challenging. We fished mostly at night because that was when the fish were biting. One night, during the tournament, while I was cutting bait, netting fish, and taking hooks out of the mouths of fish, God gave me the courage to fish. I was no longer afraid of falling in the water or touching the bait. I had a job to do, and it was not a time for fear. Little did I know that this was the beginning of my healing and restoration.

Let me admit: God told me to write this book in 2013 after being in prayer. I started and stopped writing for over seven years. I made excuse after excuse to God and to my family as to why I did not finish this prayer journal. But after I finished the book this year, God spoke to me and told me that I was right on time. You see, our God is sovereign, and nothing takes him by surprise. When he told me to write this journal, he knew that it would take this amount of time. God was well aware of the experiences I needed to walk out to make this prayer journal complete.

This excellent prayer journal contains my healing journey through prayer, fishing stories, and life experiences. I pray that you complete this entire prayer journal with an open heart to receive what God has planned for your life. And you will find the courage to do what it is God has called you to do.

Day 1

Getting to the Root

No matter how great at times, all marriages present challenges large and small, especially at dinner. After 31 years of marriage, my husband and I still have 30-minute conversations about what we want and don't want to eat for dinner. Now, I understand this is because we both have been conditioned to eat emotionally. We were both raised to "feel" like eating something. Or better yet, we need to have a "taste" for something to decide what to eat for dinner.

Let me be the first to admit that this is often exhausting. However, after having a 20-year battle with my weight, Jesus taught me how to feed my body what it needs and not just what I feel like eating; I try to get to the root of my hunger and not eat emotionally. When I choose to eat green vegetables or foods that contain fiber, protein, and other essential nutrients that my body requires daily, I feel better and have more energy and focus. I also know that I am taking care of the Lord's temple. Let me tell you, this way of thinking, i.e., getting to the root of my need for food, did not happen overnight; it took lots of prayers to change the way I thought about food.

I wish I could say that I have this same discipline in every area of my life, but that would not be truthful. There have been many times in my life, like my previous eating choices, when I needed Jesus to help me with a situation. I have been on my knees and could not articulate my needs to Jesus. So, my prayers were very surface-level and did not deal with the real issue. I began to pray general prayers about my feelings. Do you know what I mean? I would pray for things like life, health, and strength. However, in actuality, I was worried about my position at work because they were having layoffs. Instead of asking God to go before me and allow me to keep my job and give me peace in the process, knowing that he was in control, I would tell God that whatever he wanted to do would be okay with me. Well, that was not true; I would not be OK with losing my job. I knew he would cover me, but I would be emotionally discouraged, and a bit panicked.

Knowing what to ask Jesus requires us to take time to go deep into our hearts. It requires us to open our hearts and trust the God whom we serve. Sometimes, you should sit down and write about your issue—and keep writing until you get to the root of the problem.

I love the story in Luke 18:35-43 that speaks of a blind man near Jericho. He was sitting by the wayside, begging. Then, all of a sudden, he heard the multitude of people passing by. Being curious, he asked someone to tell him what was going on. Someone said to him that Jesus of Nazareth was passing by. Now, this verse could be an entire book by itself regarding our need to tell others about Jesus. But let me stay focused.

Someone had already given this man the story of Jesus and how he was healing the sick and restoring sight to the blind. Maybe he had no idea that Jesus would ever pass his way, but here was his opportunity.

When they told him that it was Jesus, he starting yelling, "Jesus, thou Son of David, have mercy on me!" He yelled so desperately that people in the crowd told him to be quiet. But the more they tried to get him to stop yelling, the more he cried out to Jesus. The blind man must have known that this was perhaps his only chance to be healed.

When we understand that Jesus is our only choice, we cry louder, pray consistently, attend church regularly, read our Bibles, and fast. But we should draw close to Jesus before our times of desperation.

While the blind man is crying out, Jesus responds to him. This is why I love Jesus; he responds to our sincere hearts. In a crowd of people, if you cry out, know that he hears you. Jesus then commands the blind man to come near.

Okay, let's pause there for one moment. Jesus is longing for us to come near to him with our hearts surrendered. He wants to speak to us on a personal level and get to the root of our hurts. Jesus is concerned about you.

When the blind man stood in the presence of Jesus, he was asked by Jesus, "What wilt though that I shall do unto thee?" Because this man was a blind beggar, he could have asked for many things. He could have asked Jesus for riches, a home, or food, which would have been a temporary fix. But it was like the man knew the root cause of his problems: his lack of sight. So, he told Jesus that he wanted to receive his sight. Understand, if he could see again, he could work and get his own money and food. Having his sight was the root of his problem, and he was clear about that fact.

The Bible says that immediately, he received his eyesight. He also began to follow Jesus and praised God. He was an example of the power of having faith in Jesus.

So, what is the root of your problem? That problem that you have been praying about for a long time? If Jesus was to visit you in the next 10 minutes, what would be your ask? Do you know the root of your issue? If you don't know, take time today to sit quietly before Jesus and ask him to reveal to you the hidden factors of your prayer request. What is the root issue causing you to not be satisfied or happy with anything in your life? Remember, Jesus is waiting on your cry.

Dear Jesus,

You are the risen Savior, and yet you want to hear from me. I know that nothing is impossible with you. You have proven your love for me over and over again. It seems that no matter how much or how long I pray, I still feel empty, or I don't have joy. I am angry, but I don't know why. Please reveal the root of my issue so I can articulate my pain. Then give me the courage to allow you to heal me once and for all.

In Jesus' Name,

Amen

Day 2

Picture Perfect

I like taking pictures, and one of my dreams is to become a good photographer. Not a great one; I would be happy with being just a good one. Taking pictures without having unacceptable background items, such as unknown people with their mouths open, is my goal. I want an image that I can post on social media with pride. To accomplish this, I would need help, so I decided to sign up for a free iPhone photography class at my local Apple Store.

When I arrived, four older ladies were already sitting at a table, talking amongst themselves. When the 20-year-old something instructor arrived, we all introduced ourselves and proceeded outside to learn more about our iPhones' capabilities. It was windy and cold out, but we were all determined to learn. The instructor began to show us "hidden" features on our phones and other excellent techniques and pointers. We took lots of pictures of each other in various lighting schemes and poses; we were excited about our newfound knowledge. I knew immediately that our families and friends would not be safe in our presence after this day. We had just enough information to be dangerous.

I will always remember one particular thing that our instructor told us. "If you want a perfect picture, you must create it." She explained that once we have our subject in focus, we should take a few seconds to look at the subject's surroundings. "If there is something in your picture that you don't want, change it." She demonstrated how we could move our camera to adjust our lighting, remove unwanted cars in the background, etc.

Change it! That is what stuck with me. Who could imagine that you could receive life lessons at the Apple Store? If you want a great picture or a great life, you have the power to change it. Jesus has given us the power of free will, which allows us to make decisions that will line up with his desires for our lives. Today, I challenge you to identify things that are in your life that you no longer want or that are not beneficial to your future. You have the ability to remove people, habits, past hurts, emotions, and any other thing that prevents you from becoming great.

Take your time, look closely at your life, don't leave anything untouched, and be truthful with yourself. Your life can be better, and you can be better. Psalm 84:11 lets us know that no good thing will our Lord withhold from us. So, ask Jesus to search your life and your heart. Is there anything that you need to remove? It's not too late; you can have a picture-perfect life.

Dear Jesus,

Today I ask you to comb my heart for anything that hinders the great life you have planned for me. I relinquish my will for your will and plans for my life. I pray for courage to change the things that I can change. I pray for you to remove anyone and anything that will prevent me from becoming who you want me to be. Without excuses or justification to others, help me to stand in truth every day. Jesus, not only do I want to have victory, but I want you to teach me how to live in victory and to not settle for anything less than a perfect picture.

In Jesus' Name,

Amen

Day 3

It's Just Not Enough

There was a time in my life when someone close to me hurt me intentionally. I felt betrayed, deceived, and taken advantage of. I didn't understand what I had done to deserve this treatment, and I thought I would never heal. After the initial hurt, I wanted a real apology. You know, not the apology you receive when someone is caught in a corner or has no other choice. I wanted a genuine, heartfelt apology. But what happens after they apologize? The hurt is still there; you are still crying and the anger—oh, the anger. You realize that the apology was good, but it didn't diminish the hurt.

In Genesis, there is a very familiar story of a man named Joseph. Joseph was the son of Jacob, and he had 11 brothers. He was loved and favored by his father. One night, Joseph had a dream that his brothers were bowing down to him. Joseph related this dream to his brothers, which made them very angry. The brothers began to plot and decided to sell Joseph into slavery. Joseph started a journey that would lead him to another country and to the house of Pharaoh.

Due to his brothers' actions, Joseph endured slavery, bondage, betrayal, harassment, and abandonment. As you can imagine, although God was with Joseph during this entire journey, he had built up anger toward his brothers who had initiated this seemingly unwanted journey.

When Joseph encountered his brothers for the first time after many years, his response was very rough. Though Joseph was no longer in prison or experiencing hardships, he was still angry. I can only imagine that all the years he spent in a dark dungeon and all the suffering that he endured came rushing to the forefront of his memory.

Joseph began to experience several emotions. He tried to find a place to cry so that no one could see him. Joseph became angry and even resorted to having one of his brothers locked up in prison. However, he could not deny that one feeling he had was love and concern for his father and his younger brother, Benjamin. I can relate to Joseph; when you have been hurt, it is often hard to control all the emotions that you are feeling. Your feelings will change several times, and that's just within the hour.

In Genesis 45:2, Joseph finally revealed himself. He attempted to reassure his brothers that he was not angry and that God had a plan for what had happened to him. Joseph understood that while people can hurt you, only God can heal you. Whatever happens to us has to go through the hands of our Almighty God. Not only does he approve of the good things that occur in our lives, but he also has to approve of the hurts and disappointments as well.

When we understand and feel as though "I am sorry" is just not enough, we must realize that God has a purpose and a plan for all our hurts. You will frustrate yourself and others trying to make yourself feel better by demanding an apology or choosing not to forgive the one responsible for your pain.

Today, I challenge you to focus on Jesus for your healing and not on an apology.

Dear Jesus,

Today I will allow you to be Lord in my life. I will release my need to punish the ones who have hurt or betrayed me. I will allow you to judge and execute punishment on those who have hurt me intentionally. Please remove my need to be right and desire for revenge. Help me to turn my heart totally to you for healing. I understand that I must choose forgiveness every day, requiring your help.

In Jesus' Name,

Amen

Day 4

Just Follow

In June of 2018, my husband, myself, and another couple went on our dream trip to Alaska for an incredible fishing adventure. We were all extremely excited to be in Alaska, amongst other great fishermen. We were on a charter boat, and Fishing began early each morning. We fished on several rivers for salmon and halibut. One day we had the opportunity to fish on the Kenai River, which turned out to be excellent. It was like fishing on a river Autobahn. The water on the river was moving fast, and boats were going at very rapid speeds to get in the other fishing boats' flow. I had never seen anything like it. Watching the boats maneuver through the river was exciting and a bit scary. However, each boat captain appeared to know precisely how to get us all safely to the middle of the river.

In my 31 years of marriage, I have learned that my husband will often use one- or two-word directives and call it communication. For example, he may say, "follow me," "don't move," or "shhhhhhh." This may work well in most marriages, but I am a person who requires explanations. I need to ask questions: "Why do you want me to follow you? What do you see?" I can't help it. I need to know. But over our years together, and the fact that I am getting older and losing my grit, I have succumbed to the short-word directives.

My husband and I fish together often, but we hunt as well, so we are often lingering in some interesting areas and terrains. I have learned to keep watch and scream when necessary. After riding the Kenai River for about four hours, the captain stopped at a little dock to stretch our legs and use the restrooms. However, the restrooms were located a short distance in the woods. When we got off the boat, my friend began walking over a small bridge to the restroom. I immediately put out my hand to stop her and explained that we should let the men go first. She had a puzzled look on her face, so I explained. I told her that I allow my husband to lead, and I will follow whenever I go into unknown territory. If a bear comes, he will get eaten first, giving me time to run. I was kidding, wink, wink. But all kidding aside, I follow because it allows him to make sure everything is safe for me.

In the first chapter of John, John was standing with two of his disciples as Jesus walks by. John then declared, "Behold the Lamb of God!" When the two disciples heard John speak, they began to follow Jesus. This is an entire message in itself about how to declare Jesus to the point that others will follow him. Okay, back to the story at hand. Jesus turned around and asked the disciples, "What seek ye?" In other words, why are you following me? They, in response, asked Jesus, "Where are you going?" Jesus responded, "Come and See."

During my Christian walk, there have been times when I walk very close to Jesus. I can hear his voice very clearly. I heed every directive that he gives, without question. My answer is yes, even before he asks anything. And in these times, I fall more in love with him.

Then, that ugly emotion called fear shows its face. These are the times when I question everything. I even doubt the voice of Jesus speaking to me. I can't see where Jesus is leading me, so I question his directives. Sometimes, I stop following all together and demand an answer before I go any further. Very grown-up, huh? Especially, since following Jesus, has never led me astray or into a dangerous situation.

If you feel like you are stagnant in your relationship or feel lost and unsure of your next step, follow him. That means reading his Word and learning how to apply it to your everyday life. Most of all, it means saying yes to him, even when you don't know where he is leading you. Follow Jesus, just like I have learned to follow my husband.

Dear Jesus,

I love and adore you. I know without a doubt that you have my best interest at heart. I am clear about the love that you have for me. You have made me feel loved so many times in my most challenging moments. Help me today to overcome fear. This emotion always shows up when I have an opportunity to trust you. Please open my eyes to recognize the onset of FEAR and acknowledge that you did not give me this emotion. I don't want to live a life of fear. Could you give me the courage to follow you?

In Jesus' Name,

Amen

Day 5

Stay on That Wall

I am one of those "make every effort to complete the task once started" type of people. It may take hours, months, or years, but I try to get it done, especially when I have a passion for the project.

Well, except for completing this prayer journal. It has literally taken me over seven years to complete. I can remember when God spoke to me and told me that my healing would come through writing this prayer journal. You would think, then, that I would get to work. I wrote about five entries and had about 25 topics in the fire. I had momentum; I was focused and had a passion for days. I am not sure what happened but after about two months, I lost interest and put it away.

One day, I went to noonday prayer at my church. As I was on my knees praying, one of the elders at our church was laying hands on everyone individually. When he came to me, he started asking God to help me complete the book, amongst other things. I began to laugh and told God "yes" again.

Here I am, over seven years later, and I have just a few more entries to complete this book. I have had to battle my mind to complete this prayer journal.

I have fought many obstacles, but the main one is my need for perfection. And, of course, doubt set in several times. "What if no one reads it?" I remember telling myself. Then I began to understand that God didn't ask me to write a bestseller or even a book that everyone would love and want me to sign. He just asked me to write the book. I had to understand that the rest was up to him. He gets the glory from my obedience.

I am reminded of a man named Nehemiah in the Old Testament, who was rebuilding Jerusalem's walls after being held in captivity. Like me, he was focused and determined to rebuild the wall. While he was working, neighboring enemies began to spread rumors about his purpose in building the wall. They also taunted him and asked him to come down off the wall and talk to them. Nehemiah sent a message back to the enemies; this is written in Nehemiah 6:3: "And I sent messengers unto them, saying I am doing a great work so that I cannot come down: why should the work cease, whilst I leave it, and come down to you?" I love the saying, "I am doing a great work, so I cannot come down."

What has God called you to do? I know that God has placed a passion in your heart for a project, task, or ministry. Like me, have you allowed others or things to stop you from completing the assignment? When I started writing again a few months ago, I felt guilty because it had taken me so long to complete this task. However, I pressed through my feelings and kept writing.

I want to challenge you today to stay on the wall! You have a great work to do, and you cannot come down. People are waiting for you to complete your assignment. Stay focused on the task at hand and no matter what happens, stay on that wall.

Dear Jesus,

I am totally in awe that you have chosen me to complete a ministry or task that will bring glory to your name. I know that you go before me, and I have nothing to fear. I have enemies who want to stop my progress, and some of these enemies live inside my head. Please help me to believe everything that you have said about me. I am available to you.

In Jesus' Name,

Amen

Day 6

Roll Away the Stone

A few years back, I felt as if I was not entirely open to God in my prayers, desires, and needs. I knew he already knew what I needed, but I felt strongly that God wanted to hear it directly from me. So, I set out to be extremely transparent with God. When I prayed, I began to be honest with him about my feelings. For example, instead of just saying, "Lord, help me," I started saying, "God, my feelings are hurt by what was said to me, and I need your healing. Lord, I feel rejected again. Please help me not to need validation from others around me to determine my worth." Praying in this manner changed my life, my prayer life. I felt closer to God, expressing my true feelings. We now have that intimate relationship that I always desired.

The Bible tells the story of Lazarus and his sisters, who were close friends with Jesus. However, they still had lots to learn and experience with him, just as I do. I have been a Christian for years, but I had a limited intimate relationship with Jesus, meaning that I would let him occupy only certain parts of my heart.

John 11 speaks of how much Jesus loved Mary, Martha, and Lazarus. Lazarus became sick and died. Mary and Martha called for Jesus to come. However, Jesus waited for two days before answering their call.

Jesus arrived on the outskirts of Bethany, and Martha ran out to meet him. She didn't wait for him to come to her house. At the first glimpse of Jesus, she ran to him and told him that he was too late. Lazarus was dead. However, though her brother was dead, Martha blurted out a statement of confidence in Jesus. Even now, if you talk to

God, he will give you what you ask. Seemingly, she understood the power of Jesus. Jesus responded that her brother would rise again. She replies, "I know that he shall rise again in the resurrection at the last day."

Have you ever been in a situation in which your faith wavered? You find yourself on a spiritual teeter-totter. You believe God and create Facebook posts and Instagram stories, declaring your total trust in Jesus' ability to correct every wrong. Then you see a small sign that things will not go your way, and you panic.

Jesus asked the sister if she believed that Lazarus could be resurrected. She responded with a safe answer—an answer that didn't require right-now faith. There are times when I ask God to heal someone, but I ask for God's will to be done—not because I want his will to be manifested, but because it's a safe prayer request, just in case he doesn't answer in my favor. Martha responded, "I know that he will rise again in the resurrection on the last day." She believed that part about Jesus. Jesus proceeded to remind her of who he was. "I am the resurrection and the life," he stated. Then he asked if she believed him. She responded with "yes" and affirmed her belief.

Moving ahead, Jesus told the sisters, "Show me where you laid him." I feel that Jesus is asking us the same thing today. He is asking you to show him your heart so that he can see where you have laid that situation that seems to be dead. He wants to see the problem you thought you would never recover from, the one you were sure would forever rest in your heart.

Opening our hearts is scary because we often equate Jesus with our friends and family members who have failed us in the past. When Jesus asked the sisters to roll away the stone, this meant, "I need you to take the first step."

Martha had a problem. Disbelief set in, as did the fear of exposing what she knew had decomposed. She knew that the body was going to smell bad; Lazurus had been dead for days. Now think about that for a moment. Sometimes our past stinks, and it's embarrassing or painful to reveal it to the Master. That is why we bury our issues and place a pretty stone on them.

Just know that it's the job of our wonderful Savior to resurrect our situations and make things right. We need to roll away the stone and allow Jesus to do what he does best: be Sovereign. That means he always has a plan. He specializes in the impossible. You can trust Jesus.

Dear Jesus,
Today is a good day for change in my life. I require healing in just about every aspect of my life. I know that my issues stink because they have been hidden for far too long. But I trust that you are healing me as I pray. Be with me while I take my first step toward healing and forgiveness. Today, I "roll away the stone" and give you full access to my heart.
In Jesus' Name,
Amen.

Day 7

Trusting Evidence

Let me say that faith is a part of fishing. I mean, there are things that you can't see at all, so you have to trust the evidence.

My husband and I fish for various fish types, but my husband loves to fish for crappie. It is a little fish, about one pound or so in weight, and it tastes good fried. He loves it so much that he will drive two hours to one of Northern California's premier lakes just to fish for crappie.

So, of course, I decided to go with him to fish for crappie one day. We went very early in the morning and were on the water by 5 am! Yes, at 5 am. Needless to say, I slept for most of the drive to the lake.

When we arrived, I woke up and gathered my belongings. Our boat was skidding across the lake within about 20 minutes of our arrival. Unlike fishing for catfish or bass, we used a small reel with a bobber on the line. Hmmm, this was new, so of course, I had questions: What is this for, and why is it so cute? My husband explained that we wanted our bait to hang in the water and not just sit on the bottom. The bopper keeps the bait off the floor of the lake, at the eye level of where the fish are swimming, so the crappie will see it and eat it. You see, unlike catfish, crappie fish are not bottom feeders.

So, I tossed my line in the water for a catch. Then I noticed that my bobber was sitting on its side. I looked at my husband's bobber, which was sitting straight up. I asked my husband what was wrong with my bobber; he explained that it was too high on my line and was causing my bait to be on the lake's floor. He also explained that the bobber revealed how the bait was being displayed under the water. So, I didn't need to see my bait; I could watch my bobber, and that would tell the story.

Often, our Christian walk requires us to believe in things that we cannot see. It is called faith. The Bible tells us that without faith, it's impossible to please God. Faith is the foundation of our salvation.

Hebrews 11:1 is the go-to scripture when it comes to talking about faith. I like the Passion Translation, which states, "Now faith brings our hopes into reality and becomes the foundation needed to acquire the things we long for. It is all the evidence required to prove what is still unseen." Okay, that part. Faith is all the evidence that is needed to prove what is still unseen. You see, faith is like my bobber. When it sits up, it's evidence of how my bait is being displayed underwater, which I can't see.

As Christians, we ask Jesus to increase our faith. The Bible tells us that faith comes by hearing the Word of God. That is because the Bible shows the character of Jesus. The more you know Jesus, the more you trust him and will obey him. So, by reading the Word, you understand the love that Jesus has for you. Then you know that you don't always have to see what Jesus is doing in your life; you trust him.

We must remember that Jesus is not like our friends and family, who sometimes disappoint us. He is trustworthy. Having faith is not just hoping or grasping at straws; it is having a firm belief that Jesus is exactly who the Bible says he is, and we build on that.

Jesus,

I praise you for all that you have done and all that you are doing for me. Thank you for working things out in my favor. Help me trust you not just when I see your hand at work but also at the times when I am not sure you hear me. I know that I can depend on you, but sometimes I have to remind myself to trust the evidence.

In Jesus' Name,

Amen

Day 8

My Wake

In 2011, my husband and I purchased our first boat, which we named the "Ashayla" after our baby daughter. It was a large blue and white Bayliner and was in excellent condition. We had been on many boats before, but this was our boat! While riding to our fishing spot, I was fascinated by the wake our boat made in the water. As my husband drove the boat, I would face the back of the boat, watching our wake and singing the theme song from "Hawaii Five-O" until my husband gave me "the look."

As we took our boat out to the water more, I learned that all the boats made wakes. The amount of wake depended on the boat's size and speed. For those who don't know, a wake is created when a watercraft moves through the water. It is also known as waves.

Creating wakes is interesting because they can cause issues for other boats. If someone is fishing or relaxing, and a big boat quickly drives by, the wake from that boat will splash water, move the fishing line, and most of all, scare away the fish. Wakes can also damage other boats if they are not approached correctly, but water-skiers use them to have a great time.

As we travel through our lives, sometimes we create wakes or waves that impact others. I thought about the story of Jonah and how he disobeyed God. God had told Jonah to go to Nineveh and preach against their sins. However, instead of going to Nineveh, Jonah went in the opposite direction, to Tarshish. His disobedience caused a very rough ride for the other occupants of the boat to Tarshish. They did nothing to deserve the boat ride they received. It was due to Jonah's disobedience and God getting his attention.

Have you ever thought about how much your disobedience impacts or sends wakes to others? The enemy will make you believe that it's your decision and that it's all about you. The disobedience of others has impacted me. I did nothing and had nothing to do with them, but their wakes came and shook my life. Many can be self-centered and will not stop to see the impact that their decisions have on innocent loved ones and others.

Understand that God has given you a responsibility to be obedient to him and his Word. You must choose to obey. The decisions you make every day impact your spouse, children, grandchildren, parents, siblings, co-workers, neighbors, etc. This is not the time to be selfish and to not think of the innocent souls around you.

But know that you can have a positive impact on others as well. If you are going to send out a "wake," make sure it will impact others' lives for good.

Dear Jesus,

I come to you to ask for forgiveness for any and every area in my life in which I have not been obedient. I know that you desire what is best for me and that you created me with purpose. I must admit that sometimes I am afraid. I am so scared of the future. I fear what others will say, I fear failure, and I fear not being good enough. Lord, help me to overcome my fears. Forgive me for any negative wakes that I have created in the village of people around me. Please give me courage and strengthen me in my weak areas. I want to be obedient to you. Lead and guide me in this next season of my life. I will place my trust in you.
In Jesus' Name,
Amen

Day 9

It Seems Impossible

I can't recall how many sermons I have heard regarding forgiveness over the years. Let me be honest and say that often I will let the sermons go in one ear and out the other. This occurred so many times because I didn't think that I needed to forgive anyone. I mean, I didn't hate anyone or wish ill toward them. However, one thing that I have learned is that God's Word will find you. All of the messages that you have heard have a way of returning to you. That is what I love about God's Word. It is there when we need it most.

When it's simple or not very impactful, forgiveness seems easy. You may think, 'Why doesn't everyone forgive?' Or, 'Why is it so hard to forgive?' But when you have been hurt so severely that it impacts your livelihood, forgiveness can be the most challenging thing. I think forgiving someone is so hard because, to do so, we must give up a part of ourselves that feels the need to stand in judgment and punish the one who hurt us. In other words, we want to play God over the lives of others.

When I finally tapped into my courage to fish, it was during a time when I was on the road to forgiveness. I had to forgive myself and others who are close to me. It was a challenging time in my life, and the road was very rocky and unsure. However, I knew that I had to forgive for my sake. I quickly understood that forgiveness is a process and that I had to choose to forgive every day until my heart healed.

When Jesus went to the cross for our sins, it was because God had a plan for forgiveness. Jesus executed that plan to reconcile us back to God.

God's plan for forgiveness should still be utilized today. Because God, Jesus, and the Holy Spirit are one, God had to send a part of himself to die to reconcile us back to himself. It is the same way for us; in our forgiveness journey, a part of us will have to die. You know, that part of us that wants revenge, or to execute judgment and punishment on the person who hurt us so deeply. Mostly, our need to be right and justified must die. This is so much easier said than done.

I am nowhere near an expert, nor do I walk out forgiveness perfectly. But here are a few things that are necessary to begin the road to forgiveness. First, you must make a clear decision to forgive. This doesn't mean that you must stay in a toxic relationship, stay at a job, or lend money again; it means that you will forgive a person for the hurtful actions taken against you. You will need to decide to forgive daily for a while. Some days you will want to forgive, and other days you will want to give that person a piece of your mind or get revenge. So, make a decision and remind yourself daily of that decision. It would be a good idea to have a trusted accountability partner during this time to remind you of your healing journey.

Another thing to do is to release your need to be right. You were hurt; you did nothing to deserve what happened to you. Go ahead and establish the wrongs done to you. This will allow you to move forward and not get stuck in grief and hopelessness. You have a choice to move on. Lastly, understand that the person who hurt you cannot heal you. Time does not heal all wounds, but God does. That is why it is possible to carry around the damage for years. Then you realize that you are not healed; you just pushed it aside. As you walk through your journey of forgiveness, God is going to heal you, just like he healed the ten lepers in the Bible. This will require you to become vulnerable and to open your broken heart to God. Let me tell you, God is trustworthy and will care of your shattered heart with tender loving care.

Walking out, forgiveness can be challenging, but it's not impossible with the God we serve. That is what makes the difference. It doesn't matter whether you want to forgive; Jesus commanded us to forgive so that he will forgive us. When we don't forgive, we judge the one who hurt us as not worthy of forgiveness, which is not our job. It belongs to Jesus.

Today, I encourage you to ask Jesus to reveal any person in your life whom you need to forgive. Ask for courage to forgive and ask Jesus to heal you of others' hurt so that you can walk in freedom.

Dear Jesus,

You are the ultimate example of walking out forgiveness. You have extended forgiveness to me so many times when I have fallen short and made mistakes. Could you help me to forgive? Right now, I must be honest and say that I don't want to forgive because I want to hold the person who hurt me accountable for their actions. Please give me the first step to forgiveness and walk with me. This hurt has impacted my daily life, and it is consuming my daily thoughts. I want freedom in my mind, body, and spirit, and you are the one who can help me. I surrender to you, knowing that you love me and that I can trust you. Thank you in advance for my healing.

In Jesus' Name,

Amen

Day 10

Know the Way

There are many benefits to being married. One of the benefits of my marriage is that my husband drives 90% of the time. The sad thing is that when I do drive the remaining 10%, I complain. Let me admit that I'm not particularly eager to drive anywhere. I was excited when my children were old enough to drive me around. At one time in my life, I had three drivers in my home, so I only drove to work. It was a delightful season in my life.

The problem with not driving is that I don't always pay attention to my husband's route to get us to our destinations. When he is driving, I usually sit back and rest, eat, talk, or sleep.

Now, let me be quick to say that my husband doesn't like taking the same route to places. He wants to change it up all the time.

A few days ago, my church was holding an event early on Saturday morning. So, my husband left for fishing before me, and I was to drive and meet him when I had completed my duties.

I placed everything that I needed in my car and started on my journey to the boat dock to meet my man for a great day of fishing. I started well; then, I began to second-guess myself. Is this my exit? I began to speak aloud, verbally. Nothing looked familiar to me. "When did they build a house on this corner?" I asked myself. The sad thing is that we had gone to this boat dock every Saturday for the previous three weeks.

After a few questions and intense stares, I kept going and found myself at the correct destination. I was a bit anxious that I had trouble getting to a place where I go almost every weekend. It was because I don't pay attention when I am not driving.

Depending on my husband to get me to a destination and not knowing my way personally is like being a Christian who depends only on a Sunday sermon or others' prayers to maintain a relationship with Jesus. Those of us raised in the church, or who have praying close family members, often rely on others' connections to Jesus to determine our walk with Christ.

You know, our parents or grandparents had a real relationship with Christ. We would see them pray and read their Word daily. However, this is not our relationship. Just because my mom had a personal relationship with Jesus does not give me a "free" card into heaven. Jesus doesn't have grandchildren, only children.

I can follow along, know the language (because I have attended so much church), make the gestures, and quote a few scriptures, but this does not equal a genuine relationship with Christ. I must know the way to get to Jesus myself. I am honestly saying that I did ride on the skirt of my mom's relationship with Jesus for many years. But after becoming an adult, I needed a one-on-one relationship with him.

So I began to cultivate my relationship with Jesus through daily prayer, fasting, and reading his Word. And it was the best decision I ever made. Jesus is now my personal Savior and Lord.

I encourage you to set aside time to intentionally develop a love and desire for an intimate relationship with Jesus Christ. You will not regret it. You have to know the way to heaven for yourself.

Dear Jesus,
I want to know you. I am not satisfied with knowing you as the Lord of my parents or other family members. I want my relationship with you. I want to know your likes and dislikes. Help me to understand your unconditional love for me. This will help me to live out my life with purpose and intention.

In Jeremiah 29:12-13, Your Word says that If I seek you with my whole heart, I will find you. I am seeking you; reveal yourself to me. Can you walk with me through life? I realize that I am nothing without you.

In Jesus' Name,

Amen

Day 11

This Seems Weird

God blessed me to be raised in a home with a prayer warrior. My mom loves to pray, and she believes in the sheer power of prayer. This is not something that has just begun in her life; she has been in love with prayer for as long as I can remember.

When I was young, I suffered from asthma and often missed school in the winter due to asthma attacks, bronchitis, or pneumonia. However, I knew that no matter how sick I was, I still had to attend noon-day prayer at my church with my mom. Sometimes I went to prayer in my PJs, wrapped in a large blanket, and laid on one of the church benches. I can remember feeling sick and having difficulty breathing. But the mothers of the church, one by one, would come and pray for me. I must admit that after the prayer, I would feel better. This helped me to understand the power of prayer in my life.

As I grew older, I settled into a habit of asking my mom to pray for me. One day, I asked my mom to pray for a situation. She told me to pray myself and reminded me that God hears my prayers just like he hears her prayers. This began my prayer journey.

I started praying daily in silence because getting on my knees and speaking out loud to Jesus seemed weird and uncomfortable. I would open my eyes every other sentence to see if anyone was looking. I can remember so many thoughts flowing through my head as I prayed: Is Jesus going to meet me here, and I fall out? Or, better yet, am I going to be late to work because I spoke in unknown tongues for 20 minutes?

I understood that prayer was an essential part of my walk with Christ, but having a desire to pray was not in my heart. I believe that it was because I felt like I didn't know how to pray effectively. I learned that counting on the prayers of others was not what I needed.

In Luke 11, Jesus spent time in prayer. After he completed his prayer, one of his disciples asked him to teach them how to pray. Jesus responded to the question with what we know as the Lord's Prayer.

Jesus gave a formula for prayer and words to say. The book of Matthew quotes Jesus as saying, "Pray in like manner." So, I believe that we don't have to say these exact words, though we must have the same intention.

What stood out to me was that after Jesus gave these words, he began a parable of a friend who required bread to entertain an unexpected guest late at night. The friend went to another friend at midnight to ask for assistance. The friend's first response was "no." He explained that he was in bed, as were his children. However, the first friend persisted. Finally, the second friend provided what was needed. Jesus then said, "Ask, and it shall be given you; seek, and ye shall find; knock, and it shall be opened unto you."

Jesus was letting the disciples know that they didn't have to pray like anyone else. However, if they asked, sought, and knocked, they would receive a response because Jesus was their friend.

After many years of being in a relationship with Jesus, I would not consider myself to be a prayer warrior by any means. However, I have a prayer life, and I talk to Jesus daily and throughout the day. I don't have one form of prayer because Jesus is too big to be placed in a box. So, I pray both out loud and in silence, and I still have beautiful prayer journals. The most important thing is that Jesus and I are in communication with one another. Now, I love spending time talking and listening to Jesus.

I challenge you to develop your prayer life today. Do what makes you comfortable while pouring your heart out to Jesus. He wants to hear from you, and he wants to give you direction for your life. If you don't pray consistently, you are missing out on a significant part of your relationship. Push through the weird feelings and spend intentional time with your Lord.

Jesus,
I am glad you call me a friend. Sometimes, I feel weird praying to you. It feels like I am just talking to myself or a wall in my bedroom. You are so busy ruling the world, so I don't understand why you take the time to hear me. I want to have a consistent prayer life with you. I will do more than talk to you only when I need something. I will come to you with an open heart to see what you need from me. I love you, and thank you for caring and loving me unconditionally.
In Jesus' Name,
Amen

Day 12

Not Like the Rest

To say that I don't have a green thumb is an understatement. My family gives me a hard time about my inability to keep a plant alive for longer than a few weeks. I am grateful for the return policy at the local growers. Yes, I am the one who will return an unidentifiable plant (or dirt with a stem) to the local growers for an exchange or refund. Let me say that it's not for lack of trying, but for some reason, I didn't inherit my mom's ability to grow anything.

When I say that my mom has a green thumb, I mean it. I have seen my mom go to one of her sister's home, find a plant she liked, and ask for a piece of the plant. She would take a sample, root not included, wrap it in a wet paper towel, place it in a zip-lock bag, put it in her purse, and take it home. Many days after "the cut" was made, my mom would place the stem of a plant in water for a few days, then plant it in a pot. In what seemed like just a few days, a full-plant would bloom.

Knowing my lack of ability to grow anything except a snake plant (which might be the easiest plant to grow), I decided to start a garden. I asked my wonderful husband to create a box garden in our backyard. One day, when I got home from work, he had completed my garden box, and it was ready for seeds. I knew that there was no turning back now.

The first two seasons of gardening were a bit shaky, but eventually, I got the hang of it. Many vegetable plants were returned to the store, and some just disappeared into the ground. However, I also produced some excellent tomatoes, green peppers, collard greens, and okra.

Because I was doing pretty well, my husband built me another garden on the other side of my backyard. I planted my okra and squash seeds in the new garden box. After about two or three weeks, I noticed many weeds and other unwanted items in the planter. I knew that I had to remove the unwanted nutrient-stealing beasts from my garden manually.

Before removing the weeds, I was worried about my ability to tell the difference between the vegetables and weeds in my garden. I didn't know how to identify my seeds at this early stage.

The next morning, I put on my pink gardening gloves and walked over to the large planter. To my surprise, I could immediately tell which item was a weed and which was a vegetable plant.

The small vegetable plants were very distinct. The leaves of the plants were starting to push through the ground. Some of them had already pushed through the dirt and were starting to grow above ground. I stopped pulling weeds to look at my plants and how they were growing. It was like they knew exactly what to do. There was something so intentional about their placement and how they were breaking through the ground. Also, their leaves were very distinct and firm. It was like they were saying, "I am doing what I was planted to do, and I will produce fruit."

On the other hand, the weeds were very flimsy-looking, and they were of various shapes and sizes. When I pulled the weeds, most of them came up quickly. Their roots were very shallow and thin.

In 1 Peter 2:9, Peter spoke to Christians scattered throughout Asia Minor (modern-day Turkey). He wanted to let them know that they would be persecuted for the sake of Christ but that they had to consume God's Word consistently to remain steadfast. Peter wanted to bring home the point that they were now chosen by God and, therefore, different from others.

As Christians, we should live lives that demonstrate that we are in a real relationship with Jesus and not just people who attend church services on Sunday mornings. This relationship is exemplified by the way we respond to life.

So, while you are reading this devotion, do a self-check of your life. Be different; be intentional about being where God has planted you. Just like the vegetables in my garden, we are to stand out clearly and boldly. We are to push through the dirt and bloom as never before.

Dear Jesus,

Thank you for choosing me to be a citizen in your kingdom. I want to be a great example of your kingdom. Let my life be different from those who do not profess a relationship with you. Please help me to endure hardship as a good soldier. Please give me the strength to endure with joy and victory rather than sadness and an attitude of defeat. Please show me the areas in which I need to become stronger and different.

In Jesus' Name,

Amen

Day 13

I Am Trying

I lived life pretty safely until I turned 40. Once I turned 40, things began to change. I started getting the courage to fish and do other things that I thought I would never do in my life. About five years ago, I began hunting. My husband is an outdoorsman and likes just about every sport, but hunting is one of his favorites. I never pursued hunting with my husband because of my fear of mice. I knew that we had to walk in fields with mice, which was not okay with me. I am not afraid of everything; I can do snakes, rabbits, spiders, and all other small animals, insects, etc. But mice and I have this understanding (can I get an Amen!).

However, because I gained the courage to fish and swim, I decided to go hunting. I got myself the cutest orange-spotted Brittany Spaniel and named him Judah. I called him Judah because if I were going to hunt, I would need to send Judah first! Judah turned out to be a good hunter. He is brilliant and understands his job. He utilizes his instincts to smell and retrieve birds, whereas I was learning and was not good. But I kept trying. My husband purchased my very first 20-gauge shotgun for my birthday. So, I practiced my shooting, and I practiced my shooting, and I practiced my shooting.

My shooting was not that great, but I loved being outdoors with my man and my buddy, Judah. I loved watching Judah run around, and then suddenly, his tail would start to wag vigorously. His nose would lower to the ground, and he would get into a pounce position. He would come to a complete stop, pointing at a hidden bird in the field. This was so fascinating; it was already inside him, as we didn't teach it to him.

(This is a message all by itself.) Anyway, after he would point, I would get my gun ready. After a command from my husband, he would flush out the bird, and I would shoot! Bang, the bird would still be flying... Bang... the bird was still flying. Then a loud BANG and the bird was coming down. I looked over only to see that my husband had shot the bird. I was not happy that I kept missing birds, but I kept trying until I could independently shoot a few birds. During my failed attempts, I could tell that my husband would sometimes get frustrated. However, I would look at him and say, "Bae, I am trying." It was frustrating for me not to have mastered this hobby quickly, but I did keep trying.

This reminds me of the story of the impotent man in John, Chapter 5. He'd had a disability for 38 years. He was not alone; many with various illnesses sat by the pool of Bethesda during a particular season and waited for an angel to come and trouble the waters. When the angel appeared, the first person in the pool would be healed. Now, I have heard this man get a bad rap in many Christian messages. I have heard that he was lazy and made excuses for not getting into the pool to be healed. As a person who has tried many things, I'd like to submit to you a different outlook.

First, he was not the only one at the pool. If there were many, and only one was healed each year, many remained at the pool or returned to the pool year after year, hoping they would be the one healed. Just a side note: What was the discussion among those who were not healed after the angel left? I mean, what could you say after the person you sat next to got healed and left, renewed and rejoicing? Year after year, you had to put on that "happy for you" face and keep waiting for your turn. Then some remained, still dealing with aliments.

Okay, back to my story. The man was at the pool for 38 years, which shows his determination and faith to be healed one day. Maybe he had nowhere else to go and no one to take him there. Just know that he had been afflicted longer than Jesus had been alive.

One day, on his way to a Jewish festival, Jesus passed by the pool. He saw the lame man and asked him, "Do you want to get well?" The lame man replied, "I am trying! I have no one to help me. I am out here trying on my own, but I keep falling short. I am just not fast enough to get to the pool, and someone always gets there before I do."

But thank God for Jesus! When we are trying our best but come up short, Jesus shows up right where we are. When Jesus shows up, he lets us know that we don't have to keep trying on our own; he does for us the things we can't do for ourselves.

I want to let you know that you should keep trying. No matter what people around you say about you, or what they believe about you and your actions, keep moving forward each day. Even if you are taking baby steps and others are making more significant progress, keep trying. Jesus will show up and make up the difference. He can do more than you ever thought could be done, changed, or elevated in your life.

Jesus,

You know I am trying. However, some days it seems that for every step I take forward, the next thing I know, I have slipped back three steps. Thank you for never giving up on me. I have faith in your love for me. I know that you know what is best for me. Please help me block out the naysayers in my life, even if that naysayer is myself. On my most challenging days, give me the strength to keep trying until you bring me a total and fantastic victory. I trust you, Jesus, with my life; that is why I will not stop trying.

In Jesus' Name,

Amen

Day 14

Hear His Voice

The most exciting thing about fishing is when I get a fish on my hook, my husband says, "FISH ON," and I jump up (literally) and grab my pole. I then reel like crazy to get my fish—all while the fish has realized its fate and is trying not to become dinner at the McKnights. It is a feeling that you must become accustomed to. Let me say that while I am reeling, it always feels like the fish is too heavy and is going to break the line and my pole, then swim away. I'll be honest: I have lost a few fish because I did not reel correctly. I would reel too hard and not reel down and guide the fish to the net that my husband was holding.

My husband started speaking to me when the fish was on the hook to help me (or maybe because he was tired of me missing fish). First, he would say, "Okay, calm down." That was because I would be screaming with excitement. After telling me to calm down, he would say, "Now reel, keep reeling, slow down, keep the pressure on the fish, now bring the fish to the net." He spoke so calmly while giving me instructions. When I am reeling in the fish, and he is speaking to me, I always tell him that I can't hear anything but his voice. It's like his voice becomes magnified in my ears.

While we were fishing in Alaska, the dock was closed to fish one day due to the weather. A nasty storm had come in, and we had to change our fishing plans. Instead of fishing for halibut, we went salmon fishing on the beautiful Kasilof River. The water is a teal color and so calming.

There we were, going downstream with our poles out, waiting to catch a big salmon in our small boat. My husband caught the first fish.

Our guide hopped out of the boat and pulled us back upstream. Then we started fishing again. My friend that was in our boat did something with her pole, and her fishing line became tangled. My husband was busy untangling her line when my pole got slammed by a fish and bent over. I jumped up and grabbed my pole, as I always do when I have a fish on it. I heard our guide telling me to start reeling. So, I started reeling my very first salmon, and I was in Alaska! As I reeled, I quickly noticed that nobody was saying anything. It was extremely quiet. Nobody was giving me instructions or helping me guide my fish. I looked over at my husband, who was still helping with my friend's fishing line. I remember becoming a bit anxious, but I kept going based on what I already knew to do. Eventually, the guide started telling me a few things, and I got the fish in. After we got off the boat, I hit my husband and asked him why he didn't say anything. He explained that he knew I could get the fish in the boat without him speaking to me. I told him that I needed his voice. I needed his guidance to make sure I didn't lose the fish. However, he again assured me of his confidence in my ability to bring in the fish without him.

In the 10th chapter of John, Jesus spoke to the Jews while he was on Solomon's porch. In verse 27, Jesus responded to the questions of the Jews, who asked him to reveal himself plainly. He stated, "My sheep hear my voice, and I know them, and they follow me." When we belong to Jesus and are in a relationship with him, we can hear him. To hear means to respond to sound or, in other words, to respond to his voice. The difference between attending church and being in a relationship with God is how you respond to his voice.

The only time hearing Jesus is problematic is when a lot of noise in your life is drowning him out. Like my husband, while fishing, you must block out all other noise (social media, friends, family), lean in, and focus on Jesus. Then allow him to develop an intimate relationship with you. Please don't ask questions, and even before he asks, let your answer be yes. Do what he has asked you to do. Read his Word and do what it says. This is how he speaks to us.

Jesus,

I want to know your voice from all other voices. Make your voice loud and clear so that I may obey. I want to be your sheep and fed from your hand daily. Please help me to conquer my fear of the unknown and put my total trust in you. I know that I need to lay down my will, but sometimes I get scared because I don't know what the future holds. Please help me to follow you and not the crowd around me. I love you, Jesus, and I know that you love me. Help me to live loved.

In Jesus' Name,

Amen

Day 15

It's Complicated

I am a fan of a movie with a good love story—the kind that leaves you feeling giddy on the inside and wanting to cuddle with your spouse. One of the films that I enjoy is "It's Complicated" with Meryl Streep, Alec Baldwin, and Steve Martin. Meryl and Alec are divorced due to Alec's extramarital affairs. And, of course, Alec marries his much younger mistress. After being divorced for ten years, Meryl has settled into her new life as a divorcee—and now Alec begins to see Meryl in a new light. Therefore, he wants her back. He realizes his mistake of leaving and begins pursuing her. Meryl has finally healed from the hurts of her past marriage and living her life. Alec is married, which causes Meryl to become confused. She begins that slope of "What If?" They begin to have an extramarital affair, and the "What If" turns into revenge on the new wife. During the "encounters," Meryl meets a friendly, stable architect, healing from his divorce, played by Steve Martin. Meryl now has a decision to make. She has to decide whether to leave the past behind and build on a relationship with Steve or continue with Alec's familiar relationship.

This is not unusual. God consistently pursues our love and a relationship with us. He wants our entire heart, mind, and soul. When you give your life to Jesus, it seems new and unfamiliar; you don't know what to expect or what he expects from you. This can cause fear or a mindset in which you retreat to your previous life—a life that is not necessarily good but familiar to you. Your enemy doesn't show you all of the pain, hard times, disappointments, etc., of your past because he wants you to remain stuck.

I received Jesus as Lord and Savior at a very early age, but I didn't always make the right decisions. So, after becoming an adult, I experienced mental and emotional battles regarding my past life and my new life with Jesus. It was a fear of the unknown and, admittedly, my lack of trust in Jesus. I didn't trust him to give me a new, better, and fulfilled life. I couldn't imagine the life that the Bible so vividly speaks about. I think I didn't know if I was worthy of having a great life. Would Jesus do it for me? Did he love me enough?

At the end of "It's Complicated," Meryl Streep must find the courage to break the ties of her past with Alec Baldwin. After she does that and assures him that they have no chance of a future, she finds herself alone again but seemingly content. One day, Steve comes by to work on her house and receives her with open arms. She was ready for a new beginning, a new relationship with adventures and whatever a relationship with Steve would bring.

Just like Meryl, we must make a clear cut with the enemy in our past. Let him know that you are no longer in a relationship with him and that he has no place in your future. Then you are available and open to receive all of what God has for you. Paul puts it well in Galatians 2:20 (ESV): "I have been crucified with Christ. It is no longer I who live, but Christ who lives in me. And the life I now live in the flesh I live by faith in the Son of God, who loved me and gave himself for me." When we die to ourselves, we have a life again because the most powerful Jesus Christ lives in us.

Dear Jesus,

Today, I admit that I have yet to turn loose certain areas of my life. I confess that I am scared and that I lack trust in your love for me. My head acknowledges your love for me, but my heart has a hard time letting go of the past and embracing your passion for me. You know the very intents of my heart, but I want to openly confess that people in my past have hurt me so profoundly that I have a hard time trusting you, the sovereign God. I am tired of living in limbo or going through the motions of a genuine relationship with you. I want the relationship with you that I sing about, talk about to others, read about in your Word, and know can exist. Today, I open my heart to you. Fill me. Then, fill me again.

In Jesus' Name,

Amen

Day 16

Superb Workmanship

In the midst of my new fishing hobby, I decided that I wanted a new boat to catch more fish. We had a nice boat, but it was huge, and we could not maneuver it in small bodies of water. I saw many people launching nice boats, and I wanted to be one of those people. I told the hubby, and I went online boat hunting. I visited several sites, compared prices and features, and read reviews.

Then I found the boat that I wanted. It was a new pleasure boat with red with gray stripes, and it was pretty. I consulted with my husband, and we decided to purchase it.

We put many miles on our boat and loved it. We have fished many, many days and nights on our boat. But after about year two, we began to notice a few flaws in our boat's workmanship. You know, things that should not happen with normal wear and tear. For example, the edges of the flooring began to come up and curl a bit. The carpet started to rip and shred in various places. Also, the bolts began to come loose from the seats. We fixed the issues that we could, but some of the things are still an eyesore. Now we have had the boat for six years, and I am sure that I would purchase from a different manufacturer if I could do it all again.

One of my favorite scriptures in the Bible is Ephesians 2:10, which states," **For we are his workmanship, created in Christ Jesus unto good works, which God hath before ordained that we should walk in them.**" I love it because Paul explains to the church of Ephesus how important and valuable they are to Jesus. He lets them know that Jesus gave his life for them and that we are chosen according to the plan of Jesus, who works out everything for his purpose and will.

In verse 10, Paul states that we are the workmanship or handiwork of God. Isn't that amazing? It's like having the perfect maker create every aspect of your life with purpose in mind. I don't know about you, but this makes me happy on the inside. There are days when I don't understand why I have this skin color, my personality, my hips, my eye color, and this brownish with a streak of blonde hair. But when God, my maker, created me, he knew exactly what he wanted me to be and how he wanted me to look.

I like God's workmanship because the older I get, the more I see His purpose manifested in my life. Each day, I have a better understanding of why he made me the way he did. I am an incredible piece of work, and so are you. You are his masterpiece, the one he placed in this world to shine so that others may see you and glorify our father or maker in heaven.

Often, people will not appreciate your value, and you will not understand your importance. Just know that we are slapping God in the face when we complain or compare ourselves to others—telling him that he did not do a great job with us.

Today, I challenge you to spend time in the mirror and thank God for everything you see, without saying anything negative.

Dear Jesus,

Well done. You created me perfectly for your purpose, and I lack nothing. I am learning to love myself as you love me. Please help me to change my mind about what I deem as flaws or defects in my life. Though I may enhance myself with wigs, nails, clothes, etc., please know that I appreciate how you made me. Bring me to my senses when I doubt my God-given natural beauty. I pray for guidance in searching out the good in my life and knowing my purpose.

In Jesus' Name,

Amen

Day 17

Trust the Process

I know what it feels like to be broken. I think many of us have walked through seasons of our lives in which we felt that we had hit rock bottom. Sometimes we hit rock bottom due to others being selfish and not thinking about how their decisions impact our lives.

Then there is that "rock bottom" that you caused by yourself. You made bad choices, one after another. Never stopping to ask God for direction or his plan, you kept going and did what you thought was best. Or you knew it wasn't right, but you kept doing it anyway. And let's be honest: You didn't pray because you knew that God would disapprove of your actions.

But what do you do after you have hit rock bottom? I mean, the damage has been done. The relationship that you put before Jesus is now broken. Your heart is aching, and you feel a deep sadness in the pit of your heart. You can feel the heartbreak every day. The tears don't stop. Waking up to a wet pillow has become the norm. Your actions did not express appreciation for the job that you prayed to Jesus to give you. Therefore, you have received your letter of termination.

The thing that I love about Jesus is his power of redemption. I have had to repent to Jesus so many times. And he is so faithful to restore me and forgive me.

The book of Ezra speaks of Israel and the process of rebuilding after they had been in captivity in Babylon for 70 years. As promised by God, it was time for restoration. They received permission and supplies to return to Jerusalem to rebuild their city and worship their God. This is a very detailed process and is discussed in several books of the Bible.

In chapter one of Ezra, Israel was given permission and supplies to rebuild their city. They were given back things stolen during the seizing of their city, such as gold and silver plates, bowls, and other items from the temple of God. The second chapter lists the exiles who returned to Jerusalem, i.e., the returning descendants. Amid this list, you find that they brought back 200 male and female singers. Yes, the praise and worship team came back with them.

Why is this so important for the rebuild? Israel knew what God required of them. They knew that God had kept his promise. The first thing that they were going to do was reestablish the worship of the almighty God. They faced opposition during rebuilding; people were discouraged, and other things happened that caused them to stop at one point. However, they were determined, and they worshiped throughout the process.

I am convinced that God cares so much more about the process than the outcome. He wants to reestablish fellowship with you during the process of rebuilding your life. Jesus doesn't want just to show you the way; he wants to walk right beside you. He wants to tell you each day that it's getting better and that you will be okay.

If you are going to rebuild, you must go back to your foundation, your relationship with God. You remember when you didn't make a move without speaking to him first. You fasted and prayed consistently. You remember when you were so in tune with the voice of Jesus that you could hear him over all the chaos of everyday life.

Today, I encourage you to go back to pure worship—not for show or fashion, but just you and Jesus. And not the organized worship that is sometimes done in our church services. But only you and him, in your bedroom, you on the floor with your eyes filled with tears of gratitude in awe of his very presence.

This season may be challenging for you; trust me, I understand. However, you have a Savior who loves you and doesn't want you stuck in this season. He is waiting for you to move closer to him so that you can feel his comfort and love.

Your first step in the rebuilding process is worship.

Dear Jesus,

I love and adore you. I am sorry for allowing the cares of the world to disrupt my relationship with you. Somehow, I lost track of you. I even lost myself. But today, right now, I want to recommit my life to you. I never thought that I would be in this place, but here I am, broken and feeling alone. As I begin to rebuild my worship foundation, I want you right in the middle of my every decision. I realize now that I am breathless without you, and I need you to breathe.

In Jesus' Name,

Amen

Day 18

Resist the Urge to Continue

First, let me say that I have a typical husband who doesn't like to take directions from anyone. It is what it is. When we travel, I know that we are really in trouble if he asks me to use the Waze app for a brief moment to find our way.

One rainy day, while driving home from a homegoing celebration for our uncle, we were hungry and tired from the day of activities. My Waze app was on, guiding us in getting home as quickly as possible and avoiding the 4 o'clock traffic from Hayward to Sacramento. While we were driving, the app told us to get off the freeway at a specific exit. The app doesn't tell you why; it just gives you directions. However, it does tell you that you will save five minutes.

So, we got off and took the suggested route. We continued on the proposed path, which took us under the freeway. We could see that a car accident had occurred and slowed down traffic on our usual route.

We almost didn't follow the directions to exit when we did. We had to make a decision: keep going the way we "knew" was right or trust the Waze app and its knowledge of what was ahead of us?

In case you are not aware, the Waze app utilizes routes and information from other drivers on the road to get you quickly to your destination. It already knows what is ahead of you.

Even knowing this, you must resist the urge to continue with what you know versus following the app's directions.

This is like our relationship with Christ. There are things in our lives that we need to stop doing so that we can follow Christ. However, resisting the urge to continue is tough. What we are doing is familiar and safe, and we know the outcome.

But what if we resisted the urge to continue doing the same thing and followed God's plan? You know, resist the urge to continue eating unhealthy foods, the urge to keep spending time with non-believers hoping for a Godly relationship, the urge to keep being late for worship, or the urge to keep complaining about the goodness of Jesus?

You must trust Jesus and get the courage to try something new. Trust that he has the best in store for you.

In Matthew 2:12, the angel told the wise men to go home another way after seeking the baby Jesus. Sometimes we are leaning toward the normal, what is familiar. However, we must resist the urge to continue what we are doing; we must go the way God has explicitly ordained for our lives.

I challenge you to step out on faith today and allow Jesus to show you a new, better way. Don't worry; he will not leave you. He is right there with you every step. It would be best if you resisted the urge to continue with your regular life.

Jesus,

I ask you to help me do it differently this time. You know my "it." The thing that doesn't allow me to surrender to you. The "it" that I know is not your will for my life. I want the courage to break generational cycles of abuse, fornication, alcohol, drug addiction, abortion, anger, unforgiveness, and low self-esteem, to name a few, from my life. I know that there are actions that I need to take, but I also know that there are things that only you can remove or help me handle. So, I declare my trust in you. I believe that you are everything that your Word states about you. For this reason, I will resist my urge to continue with my life as it is and will follow you instead.

In Jesus' Name,

Amen

Day 19

Take It to Jesus

There is a man mentioned in Luke 9:41-43 in the Bible. Jesus had just come out of the mountain, being transfigured, and a crowd of people was waiting for him. Word had gotten out about Jesus healing the sick and performing miracles.

In this crowd, a father came forth out of love and desperation for his son and spoke directly to Jesus. While he had Jesus' attention, the man explained that a demon was causing his son to have seizures. The young boy screamed and often went into convulsions, all while foaming at the mouth. The father spoke from his heart and said that the spirit was destroying his son. He mentioned that he had asked the disciples to pray, but nothing happened.

Jesus rebuked the crowd and his disciples, then asked the man to bring his son to him. While the father was getting his son to Jesus, the spirit threw the boy to the ground and caused him to have a convulsion.

What comes next is the part that I love. When Jesus saw what was happening, he immediately rebuked the impure spirit, healed the boy, and returned him to his father.

I am sure that I am not alone in saying that I have stepped up and gone to Jesus with my issue. I want you to know that you can and should take everything to Jesus in prayer. Don't allow desperation to set in before deciding to take it to the one who can solve it. What I love about Jesus is that you can take your hurts, your challenges, your areas of weakness, and your past to him for restoration and healing. Nothing is too big or too small for Jesus.

What caught my attention about this story is that the impure spirit tried it one last time. Before the son could get fully in the presence of Jesus, the spirit threw him to the ground. I can only imagine that the demonic spirit knew that if the son were to reach the presence of Jesus, he would have to leave and find another home. The spirit recognized the power of Jesus and that he was no match for it.

Praying for family members who don't seem to be changing is hard, but don't give up. The enemy is aware that you are taking your loved one to Jesus, and he knows what will happen. The impure spirit in your loved one—that spirit of lying, stealing, fornicating, adultery, pride, etc.—understands that it cannot stay if they are in the presence of Jesus.

In 1916, an African-American Methodist minister named Charles A. Tindley composed a song called "Leave It There." This song has been sung in many churches over several generations. One of the lines says, "Take your burden to the Lord and leave it there." This is a must for Christian believers; let's take our burdens to Jesus and leave them there.

I encourage you to take time to create a detailed list of areas, specifics, and people you need to take to the Lord. Be very specific—and whatever you do, don't stop praying and believing. Leave it with Jesus.

Jesus,

You are amazing. I have personally experienced your goodness and favor in my life. I remember times when I was not in a relationship with you, yet you kept loving, providing for, and guiding me. Now that I am in a relationship with you, I know you would not withhold any good thing from me. I feel your love every day when I awaken from sleep. Jesus, there are things that I am currently struggling to overcome. No matter what I do, these issues and concerns do not go away. I have prayed before, but I am not sure that I believed when I prayed. Help my areas of unbelief. I want to trust and acknowledge that you love me enough to answer my prayers.

In Jesus' Name,

Amen

Day 20

Take a Rest

The older I get, the more I find myself acting like my mom. One of the many traits that she passed down to me was the gift of "always moving." In fact, my mom got this trait from my grandmother, whom we would often visit in Guthrie, Oklahoma. (You will need a good map to locate it.) During our visits, I would sleep on the couch in the living room. I remember lying there, tired and wanting to sleep, but watching my grandmother go from her room to the kitchen, to the bathroom, back to her room at least five times. Then she would proceed to "do stuff" in her room for another hour with the lights on.

Well, my mom is the same way, and then there is me. I very seldom sit and watch a movie or a full game of football. I am always moving and shaking around my house. I will feed the dog, clean out the fridge, wash all linens, vacuum, clean out the car, etc. If I sit down, I am working on church social media, reading a book, or writing a book. Anything I can find hands to do, I will do. And for some reason, I never run out of things to do.

Recently, on a Saturday afternoon, I took a nap. My daughter was so surprised that she posted on Facebook, and I quote, "God is moving, my mom is taking a nap!" I laughed, but it made me think about the importance of resting. My family is always telling me to sit down or to get some rest.

In Matthew 11:28, Jesus speaks of having rest: "Come unto me, all ye that labour and are heavy laden, and I will give you rest." When Jesus calls you to a task, it may seem strenuous or heavy to people looking from the outside. However, when you are yoked up with Jesus, you can actively work and be at rest at the same time. This is because you are walking in step closely with Jesus, and he has already done the hard work. He is providing direction and guidance. You must be obedient and go the way that Jesus has spoken to you.

I have learned that you don't always rest by sitting on the couch, going to the spa, and taking a vacation. I have done these things and was still overwhelmed, frustrated, and unhappy.

The ultimate form of rest is being yoked with Jesus, who is aware of your labor capacity. The problem with us ladies is that we take on things that God never intended. We join groups, take classes, relocate, change positions, all without consulting Jesus. I have learned that just because I can do something doesn't mean that it's my job to do it.

There is an unexplainable rest in the will of God. If you have unexplained frustration or anger, talk to God. Make sure that you are yoked up with Jesus. That means walking where he walks and leaning into him for support.

Dear Jesus,

Thank you for your Word, which leads and guides me. I am not sure what is going on in my life, but I can't seem to find rest. I can't seem to make things in my life fall into place. The more I do, the more I appear to be falling behind. I am desperate to know and walk out your will for my life. I admit that I have taken on tasks that you did not ordain in my life. I can no longer live at a stressful pace. Please solidify your Word in me and give me rest. I am exhausted, and I need your help. I am open to receiving what you have for me. This time, I will obey.

In Jesus' Name,

Amen

Day 21

The One

To say that my husband and I often fish is an understatement. On any given Saturday, you will find us on a river or lake with our poles in the water. Fishing drew us closer together, and we have fun doing it.

Sometimes, I sit back and laugh at myself. I would never have thought that I would be fishing and loving it. My husband and I have had so many encounters and we laugh while waiting on the fish to bite.

One early Saturday morning, we were going catfishing in our favorite spot. It is our favorite spot because we are pretty much guaranteed to catch fish. This spot is a 45-minute boat ride from the boat dock. Because the ride is so long, and because we have done it so much, we go into "auto" mode as we are driving. Let me be honest; most times, I go to sleep while my husband drives the boat.

On this particular Saturday, I was sitting and listening to music while my husband drove the boat. About halfway to our destination, I noticed that a sheep had fallen in the water close to the bank. Unfortunately, he had already drowned. This is not an unusual sight for us. In the past, we have seen sheep, a cow, and a goat floating in the water. So, when I saw it, I told my husband, "Awww, it's a dead sheep."

When we went a bit farther, we saw a man frantically waving his hands on the bank. My husband stopped the boat so that we could hear what the man was saying. He was in distress and very frantic. The problem was that he didn't speak English very well. He was pointing at the water and saying "sheep." He was also carrying a rope. It was clear that he wanted us to help him get the dead sheep out of the water. So, we turned the boat around and went back to the dead sheep. The farmer tossed me the rope, and my husband (because I was not touching a dead sheep) placed the rope around the dead sheep's neck.

The farmer began to pull the sheep up the bank. A few seconds later, another farmer came with a cart, and they placed the sheep on it. Then the farmer started pointing and saying "sheep" once again. He was telling us that another sheep was in the water on the other side of the river. My husband and I started driving. Then we spotted the sheep. He was still alive under some brush but was barely holding on. We moved to the farmer, got the rope again, and then went back over to the sheep. This sheep was tangled in tree limbs and could not get free. Again, my husband wrapped the rope around the sheep's neck. (Apparently, I will not touch a live sheep, either.) He gave me the rope as he began to untangle the sheep. We then took the sheep across the river. I was driving, and my husband was holding the rope so as not to drown the sheep. We got to the bank and I tossed the rope to the farmer and his helpers. They thanked us, and we went on our way.

As we went a little farther down the river, we noticed about 50 or more sheep standing on the cliff's edge overlooking the river. A few of the sheep had climbed down the cliff to drink water from the river. When we passed by on the boat, we startled a few of them, and they ran back up the bank. I said to my husband, "Oh, my God, he is going to let the rest of the sheep drown while he is worried about the other two sheep." We went on to our fishing spot and caught a few catfish for the day.

For some reason, the 50-sheep scene remained in my mind for a few days. Why would the farmer leave the entire flock of sheep to save the other sheep? It was irresponsible, I thought. Then the Lord reminded me of the parable of the Lost Sheep in the 15th chapter of Luke. This farmer was not irresponsible; he was a good shepherd.

In the 15th chapter of Luke, Jesus is being taunted by the Pharisees. The scribes asked him how he could receive and eat with sinners. Jesus, in his wisdom, responded in a way that, hopefully, they would understand; he spoke in parables. Jesus spoke of three things that were lost: a sheep, a coin, and a son.

In the parable of the sheep, Jesus talked about a man who had 100 sheep and who lost one of them. He clarified that the man would leave his 99 sheep in the wilderness and go searching for the lost sheep. This demonstrates the importance of every sheep in this man's life. The man would look for his one lost sheep and celebrate once that sheep was returned to the fold. He would call for a celebration with his friends and neighbors and declare that his lost sheep was now found.

Then Jesus explained the parable by saying that heaven rejoices over one sinner who repents. He was saying how vital every soul is to him. This is why, when we were lost in our sins, Jesus made every effort to find us and bring us back to him.

Even when we get lost, time and time again, Jesus searches for us and finds us. He is not mad or frustrated; he only wants us back in his care.

Jesus,

Thank you for searching for me when I was lost in my sins. I was scared and afraid and I didn't have a clear path in my life, but then I saw you. You never gave up on me. I know that heaven rejoiced when I returned to you. I understand that I am important to you and that you love me unconditionally. Sometimes, I feel that I was not worth finding, but you keep searching. I don't know what the future holds for me or what you have planned for my life behind the scenes, but I will be obedient to your Word. I am going to wait for you to give me my next direction. Thank you for loving me.

In Jesus' Name,

Amen

Day 22

Say What?

God has given me—or I picked up—the gift of talking. I remember getting good grades on my report card when I was younger, but "excessive talking" would be written in the comments. My mom had threatened me about my talking, so one day, when I was in sixth grade, I was trying very hard to not say a word. I wanted to say something to my friend so badly. I was that child who made friends with all of the students, and I could and would talk to anyone. Needless to say, my talking would get me in trouble with my teacher.

One Sunday night, I was about 12 years old during our Young People Willing Workers (YPWW) class, we were discussing our speech and how what we say impacts others and that Jesus is listening. We began talking about whether cussing was a sin. My teacher, Elder Martin Gettis, told the class that cussing was for people who didn't have anything to say; cussing was just filler words. That was it for me. That night, I made up my mind that I would not cuss because I would never run out of words to say. I would be able to express myself without using filler words.

As I grew older, my words were less excessive, but they turned offensive. They were offensive because I would not cuss, but I could tell you off without saying one cuss word. The problem with this was that I came across as very cold and unapproachable, and that is not who I was on the inside.

I kept this mindset until the Lord reclaimed me when I was in my twenties. However, by this time, the way I spoke to others was not seasoned with grace. I would say what was on my mind with no regard for the other person's feelings.

As I grew in my spiritual walk and ministry, I learned that I was hurting more people. I remember getting a phone call one day to tell me that I had made a statement to a young lady that had made her cry. I was shocked, and I felt terrible.

In the fourth chapter of Ephesians, Paul spoke to the church at Ephesus and gave them a list of things they needed to change in their lives if they were going to be followers of Christ. Like us, they had to live in a way that reflected their new status as Christians. He told them to live worthy of their calling, keep the unity of the Spirit, and grow in maturity.

Ephesians 4:29 states, "Let no corrupting talk come out of your mouths, but only such as is good for building up, as fits the occasion, that it may give grace to those who hear." This scripture, as you can imagine, really hit home for me.

I am glad that I responded to the conviction of the Holy Spirit in regard to my mouth. I started praying before I spoke and imagining myself in the other person's shoes. Lastly, I asked Jesus to change my heart. And just so you know, I did apologize to the young lady.

Today, I challenge you to pay close attention to the words you say to others. Are you edifying and encouraging? Or are your comments tearing down, destructive, and hurtful? If you are like me, you need to do some soul searching.

Jesus,

Could you help me with my mouth? Sometimes, I can't believe what comes out of it. I have been hurt many times by others' words, and it didn't feel right. I am still healing. Don't let me be the person who hurts others with thoughtless words. This includes the words that I speak to my spouse, children, and close family members. I want to be that person who positively

impacts the lives of others. And I don't want anything to come between my relationship with you. With your help, my change starts today.
In Jesus' Name,
Amen.

Day 23

What Do You Know?

Oprah Winfrey has a monthly magazine that contains excellent information. It talks about recipes, travel suggestions, clothing, and, of course, Oprah's favorite things for Christmas at the right time of year. The article that I like reading the most is a section entitled "What I Know for Sure." In this article, each month she discusses one thing that she knows for sure—the thing that can't be changed, the thing that she has learned or experienced and that will stick with her forever.

I believe that we should all have some things that we know for sure—something that we have experienced personally, and no one can tell us anything different. I would call it "knowledge of the heart." It's not necessarily what you were taught growing up, but it's an undeniable experience. A "heartfelt truth" is another good name for it.

Psalm 48:10 states, "Be still and know that I am God." This is an excellent passage of scripture on which we can all meditate daily. I believe that this scripture will come alive in the most challenging times of our lives. You need to know when to move and when to allow God to be God and move on your behalf. And can I say that it is hard to be still when you are not sure of what God is planning behind the scenes for you?

When I was growing up, during the summertime the neighborhood children would often play in the streets after dark due to the extreme heat in the day. Sometimes, while we were playing, a stray dog would come out of nowhere and chase us. One time, while a dog was chasing me, my brother told me to stand still and not run. 'Are you crazy?' I thought, and I proceeded to jump on top of my mom's yellow Toyota. I had heard that you should not run from dogs, but I didn't know if that would work for me. And let me be honest, I would not trust it and risk being bitten by the dog. My flesh was at stake.

There have been times—many times, actually—when, instead of being still and allowing God to be God, I put my hands in it. I spoke when I should have kept quiet. I went versus staying at home. I sent the email when I should have just continued to watch my Hallmark movie. I know that I am not alone in this awful habit.

But then I started not just reading about God but also experiencing God. A trust relationship with my Savior began in my heart and mind. I started not only reading his Word but also living out his Word. And that made the difference. My trust in God grew. The confidence that I have developed with God allows me to be still and know, without a doubt, that God loves me, and I don't always have to make a move. This trust allows me to be still and watch God work on my behalf. I mean, I can be still and watch him orchestrate a victory on my behalf that I could never have imagined.

I can be still with the full confidence that God is working on my behalf because I rest in the knowledge that he has gone before me and prepared a way for me. Because I am in a relationship with God, he has shown that he cares for me and wants me to succeed and prosper in every aspect of my life.

Do you trust God enough to be still and know? What about God: Do you know for sure?

Dear Jesus,

Your love for me is constant and never-ending. This is one thing that I know for sure. I love that I never have to wonder about your love. There are areas in my life in which I can be still and know that you are coming to my rescue. However, there are also areas in which being still is scary for me. I try to be still, and when I don't see you working, I get antsy and start making moves independently. Lord, teach me how to wait on you. Let me trust your love for me.

In Jesus' Name,

Amen

Day 24

Knowing the Difference

At the risk of being dismissed from the fishing community, I want to say that fishing is deceitful in so many ways. I know this is not what the fisherman's society wants you to know, but someone had to say it. After I gained the courage to fish, I quickly learned that there was an art to it. I am a girly girl, and I like things that are pretty. I like flowers, ribbons, and bows. To my husband's dismay, when I began to fish that did not change. When we went to a sporting goods store to shop for tackle for fishing, I would pick cute things. I had a pink fishing pole and reel set-up that was adorable. I was not sure if I would catch fish, but I would be cute while trying. I also chose pink and green lures and other colorful swimbaits. Soon my husband gave up trying to change me.

I quickly learned that you want your bait or lure to mimic what a fish would naturally eat or attack when you fish. That is why lures and baits come in different sizes, shapes, colors, and even smells.

Let's take the lure, for example. The name is perfect because your purpose is to "lure" the fish to your bait without seeing the hook inside of it. To lure the fish, you must find out what you are attempting to mimic. I often fish with a pink and green worm. I chose the worm because it was cute (yes, I did). I started catching a lot of bass using this lure, but I didn't understand why. Then, while watching a fishing show, I learned that the pink and green lure mimics baby trout, which is what bass eat.

Not only is it essential to pick the right lure, but to get an unsuspecting fish to bite, you must make the lure maneuver like live bait while in the water. For example, when my pink and green worm is in the water, I let it float to the bottom. Then I make jerking motions to make it look like a baby trout in trouble. I know, I know, it's not right, but I want to catch fish, and I love it.

In 2 Corinthians 11, Paul warned of counterfeit apostles—deceitful workers masquerading as apostles of Christ. He went on to say that they do this because Satan himself masquerades as an angel of light. Because Satan himself does it, we should not be surprised. Paul reminds us that, in the end, they will be exposed for their behavior.

As Christians, we don't want to be deceived and walk out of the will of God. Therefore, we must be able to identify the works of the enemy. The only way to do that is to get closer to God to learn his characteristics, likes, and dislikes. Developing intimacy with God is a must. That means opening our hearts totally to him and allowing him to show us things about him that we would not know or understand otherwise.

Let's be clear; satan is doing everything in his power to lure us into his trap. He disguises jobs, spouses, food, money, peace, and freedom in front of us. Then, once we go after these things, we find out that they are not what they seem. They were lures, and they were fake; we have been deceived. However, if we walk with Jesus and learn his ways, he is the light that guides us. He exposes the plan of Satan through his Word. That is why the enemy doesn't want us to spend time in his Word.

Dear Jesus,
I am so glad that I am in a relationship with you. I know that you are for me and not against me. You have my best interest at heart. There are a few areas of my life in which I am blind and confused. I need your help and guidance in exposing the plan of the enemy. Please make your will for my life, direct and clear. Don't let me fall prey to Satan and his schemes. Please give me the courage to change my life and totally surrender to you.
In Jesus' Name,
Amen

Day 25

Going With the Flow

I never knew that fishing could be so detailed and complicated at times. Although fun and relaxing, it is definitely a sport. One of the many things that I had to learn was the tide tables. Simply put, this is when the water moves out to the ocean, thus low tide. Then, after a few hours, the water returns to the rivers and sloughs, i.e., high tide. The best time to fish is when the tides are moving out or in. That's because the water's movement causes the bait to move, which, in turn, causes the big fish to come out and eat. That is my simple version of what happens. I am sure it is more scientific than that, but hey, I am new at this.

One early morning, my husband and I arrived at our "spot" on the river. My husband stopped the boat and waited. He looked at the water to determine whether the tide was coming in or going out. He decides this because the tide will turn our boat in the direction of the tide. Another way to determine the direction of the tide is to look in the water. Suppose you see leaves, trees, shrubs, and other items floating downstream; you know that the tide is going out. We have seen a dead cow—yes, a cow—floating downstream, which helps you understand the water's power.

The direction of the tide determines how we fish. We want our bait to do what is naturally done underwater. Interestingly, when we fish for a few hours, we see things in the water that go out; then, in just a matter of time, the same leaves, trees, and shrubs return. When I first learned about the tides, I found them fascinating. It also proved to me just how amazing God is, and his creations are past our understanding.

Paul wrote a letter to the church at Ephesus. I love the book of Ephesians in the Bible because, in it, Paul reminds us of how much God loves us and about the sheer power of Jesus Christ in our lives. In the 4th chapter of Ephesians, Paul wrote to the church in Ephesus, reminding them to stay strong. He encouraged them to walk worthy of their calling and live lives of character, moral courage, and personal integrity. He told them to express gratitude to God for their salvation. Humility, gentleness, patience, and bearing one another should be characteristics of all believers' daily lives.

In verse 14, Paul reminded the church to grow and mature in Christ. Like the tides in the river move items in the water, he told them not to be tossed to and fro, carried about with every wind of doctrine. In other words, they should not be so easily moved down the river. They should not allow the craftiness of men to sway them to the left or right.

Know what you believe about Jesus and stand on it. Your belief in Jesus comes through learning his Word, through reading, and living His Word. You must spend time in God's Word daily. This is how you can determine what is true and what is a lie. If you question a doctrine, you can put it under the lens of the gospel. If it lines up with God's Word, you know that it's okay to follow. However, if you don't know God's Word, you are subject to accept anything. This will cause you to go upstream and downstream with no stability.

What do you believe about God, about Jesus Christ and the Holy Spirit? It is essential to study and stand on what is true.

Going with the flow will not land you in the will of God for your life.

Dear Jesus,

Thank you for being with me through all of my tough times—the times when I didn't acknowledge your presence in my life. Lord, I ask you not to give up on me. I want to be better. I want to grow. Allow my faith to anchor in your

Word. This is the only way my life will be stable. I am coming to you with an open heart, ready for change, prepared for something tangible. Can you help me to stop going with the flow in life? I know you are what I need most in my life.

In Jesus' Name,

Amen

Day 26

Following Directions

I grew up with three older brothers and one younger sister in the streets of Wichita, Kansas. I am a self-proclaimed "tomboy." I loved nothing more than to play a good game of "tackle the man" with the football in my mom's living room. This game consisted of a ball (a sock rolled up with rubber bands) tossed in the air and retrieved by the one who wanted to be tackled. Growing up, I often played basketball, baseball, and other sports with my brothers.

My being a tomboy was not what my mom had envisioned for her firstborn daughter after birthing all boys. I am sure she had visions of passing down her excellent sewing skills, cooking, cleaning, and other "dainty" things to me. But that was not me, and I had to be outside with my brothers. I, however, did pick up a love for baking. To this day, I love baking cakes, cookies, and pies.

I must have been about 12 years old when my love for baking flourished. I had an issue in that I was too impatient and wanted, at the same time, to bake and play a basketball game on the two traffic signs (a stop sign and a school crossing sign) posted outside our house.

While making a chocolate Betty Crocker cake, I read the instructions on the back of the box and decided to alter them for my convenience. I turned up the oven a few degrees so the cake would bake faster, thereby allowing me to continue with my outdoor activities. This was not the first time that I had decided not to follow the instructions of a recipe clearly printed on the back of the box. About 70 to 80% of the time, the outcome was not in my favor. My desserts would come out runny, not done in the middle, hard, burnt, or just plain wrong. After wasting groceries and seeing my frustration as to why my attempts at making desserts were not successful, my mom felt that I had been through enough—or she wanted me to stop wasting money.

In her sanctified voice (soft but firm), my mom explained to me, "Kendria, don't you know that the people at Betty Crocker have staff members who have cooked this cake hundreds of times to get the time, temperature, and order of the recipe correct?" She told me that the workers at Betty Crocker had done the hard work for me. "You don't have to guess, experiment, or change anything. If you follow the recipe, the cake will come out perfect every time." Ouch!

This story brings to mind the story of David in 1 Chronicles 14, in which the Philistines heard that David had been anointed king over all Israel. The Bible says that the Philistines went looking for him in full force. When David heard they were looking for him, he went out to meet them. Then David inquired of God, "Shall I go up against the Philistines? Will you give them into my hand?" God responded with a "yes" on both accounts. So, David and his men defeated the Philistines. According to verse 13, the Philistines came up against David again. Once more, David inquired of the Lord. This time, God gave different instructions to David. He told David to go around and come against them opposite the balsam trees. God then told David to wait until he heard marching in the tops of the trees; then, it would be time to go to battle. God told David that he had gone out before him to strike down the army of the Philistines. The Bible then says (unlike me with my baking) that David did exactly what God had instructed.

We live in a "do you, boo" society, and everyone is doing what is right in their own eyes. This mentality should not be named among believers, as we must seek the face of Jesus for direction. We must trust God's specific divine plan for our lives daily. Following directions when it comes to God is vital. You can't circumvent his plan and expect things to work out for your good. Sometimes we don't understand what God is doing, and frequently it just doesn't make sense. But understand that God has gone before you to make your pathway clear to defeat your enemies. We often take matters into our own hands because we are unclear or fearful or don't like the plan that God has revealed to us. We don't see how God's plan will make us happy down the road.

Having confidence in our amazing God and his plan for you will make your life so much easier. We often say that we have faith in God, but our actions and words speak differently. There comes a time in every believer's life when you must acknowledge and confess that you either do or don't trust God. Don't live in denial any longer. If you do some soul searching and find that what you have is not total confidence in God, ask him to change your heart. This is the most significant step in your relationship with him. How can you obey him if you don't trust him?

Dear Lord,

I must admit that there are areas in my life where I lean to my own devices and understanding. I am making decisions about my life based on my feelings and the things I hear and see. I have not consulted you about this season of my life. I am often fearful of the answer that you are going to give me. Your responses or plan don't always line up with my desires and wants. I know that you have my best interest at heart. Please renew my mind today. I pray for full confidence in you and your plans for my life.
In Jesus' Name,
Amen

Day 27

Overcoming Fear

I blame my mother. I love my mom very much, but she is why I had an extreme fear of water—or, more precisely, swimming. I can remember the event like it were the year before last. When I was about six years old, my family and I went to a neighborhood swimming pool to stay cool and have some family time. My mom and brothers were all in the pool, swimming and playing around. Now, my mom is an excellent swimmer. I remember her swimming, doing the backstroke and floating, while I was on the side of the pool, watching.

Everyone was having a great time, but there I was, sitting with the other non-swimmers. My mom flagged me to come to her. Let me explain that, back in my day, when your parents spoke, you obeyed without question or hesitation. So, when my mother beckoned for me to come to the side of the pool, I did so with tears in my eyes because I knew what she wanted, and fear had already gripped my heart. When I went to the end of the pool, she told me to get in the water. I explained that I was perfectly fine on the sidelines, watching my brothers and friends from the lovely seats. She would not take no for an answer. Not only did she want me in the water, but she also wanted me to jump in. I am sure today this would be an open case with Child Protective Services. So, there I was, standing at the edge of the swimming pool, with my mom's arms stretched out for me. She assured me that she would catch me and that I had nothing to fear. I trusted my mom. Why should I not trust her? She was my mom, a youth leader in the church, and a licensed missionary. I remember taking a deep breath, bending my knees, closing my eyes, and jumping. The next thing I knew, I was underwater in a full panic. I couldn't breathe. I was dying—or at least, I thought. Then I felt my mom pulling me up and laughing, yes, laughing. I was coughing up water and crying at the same time. She said to me, "See, you are okay." Well, I was not okay. I was traumatized for the next 30 years of my life.

Fear is impactful because one traumatic event can impact the rest of your life, if you allow it. You can think that you have overcome or put something behind you, and then, at the most inopportune time, it rears its ugly face. However, I have also learned that fear can lay dormant and subtly do its ugly work, just enough to cause you to not move or go forward.

When God gave me the courage to fish, I had to face my fear of swimming or drowning. This was because we fished on a boat, in the middle of a body of water. I was aware that I couldn't fish and worry about falling in the water simultaneously. So, I prayed about my fears and asked God specifically to help me overcome my fear of the water. And God did it over time because now I fish with my focus on the fish and not the water.

One day, my son told me that the Lord spoke to him and said, "Make Fear Homeless." Somehow, I knew that this word was for me to apply in various areas of my life.

When God told me to start a publishing company, Make Fear Homeless Christian Publishing was born.

What fears are keeping you from becoming everything God wants and has planned for you? Is it a fear of failure, a fear of being hurt, rejected, or disappointed? Don't be ashamed of your anxiety. Instead, your first step to healing is admitting your fear. After you acknowledge your fear, ask God to remove it. Please don't play with it or allow it to remain in your life any longer.

One thing that I have learned about fear is that it grows. It can begin in one area and then spread to other areas of your life. You will need the courage to go face to face with your fears. If you allow him, God will walk with you while you stand toe to toe with your worries.

I took swimming lessons three years ago—and, yes, I put my head underwater! I was so excited, even learning to swim with people half my age. That is a victory, my friend.

Dear Jesus,

Thank you for creating me for greatness. All that I am is found in you. You have never left me to conquer fears by myself. I know that you are actively working out things on my behalf. Could you help me to trust you more? Fear has caused me to miss opportunities, advancements, happiness, joy, and other things that I know you had planned for me. I know that you have not given me the spirit of fear, so help me recognize any fear in my life. I want to be free.

In Jesus' Name,
Amen

Day 28

Time With Jesus

I come from a long line of church workers, and I have attended church literally all of my life. My family members are not just church members; they are church workers. Following my mom's and grandmother's footsteps, I have been in just about every ministry in the church, from choir to usher board. I grew up in an era when parents didn't ask you what you wanted to do in the church; they told you and signed you up. So, some of the ministries I was involved in when I was young were definitely not my calling.

After becoming an adult, I learned to serve wherever there was a need in the church, mostly when I was a member of smaller churches. The problem with this mentality toward ministry is that you can find yourself overwhelmed and involved in ministries that God did not call you to do. There have been times when I served in so many ministries that my relationship with Jesus was fading because I had no time for him. It was so bad that, even when I was attending church, my focus would be on others having an experience with Jesus and not worshiping my Savior.

This reminds me of the familiar story of Mary and Martha in Luke 10. Jesus and his disciples entered the home of Martha, who welcomed them. This is just like me doing ministry; I would receive Jesus, but what I did once he came in was the problem. I would lead the church in worship; then, I would make sure everyone was ready for the remainder of the program. This was important, but not as important as resting in the very presence of Jesus. Martha's sister Mary was there, and the Bible states that she sat at the feet of Jesus while he taught his disciples.

Let me add that I was lost and needed direction during this season of my life. If only I had taken the time to sit at the feet of Jesus and be taught unapologetically, as Mary did. I always admire believers who intentionally have intimacy with Jesus right in the middle of church service. They are focused on why they are at church, and they want to see, worship, and experience Jesus for themselves. They appreciate all of the various ministries in the church and the duties required, but they are determined to steward the presence of Jesus and not allow this time to pass them by. Although Jesus lives in our hearts, and we can always talk to him, there are times when he will manifest himself with power. This is the time to stop "church work" and sit at his feet.

The Bible states that Martha was distracted by all of the preparations that had to be completed for her company. This caused frustration to set in her heart—and I can fully comprehend her feeling. I have experienced frustration many times while serving in the church. Like Martha, I look at others around me, who are seemingly doing nothing, and I tell Jesus about it in prayer.

Martha then proceeded to "tell on Mary," only for Jesus to explain that Martha was worried about a lot of unnecessary stuff. What Mary was doing was needful.

I have come to learn that sitting at the foot of Jesus is needful. Why? Because we must sit in his presence and receive directions for the next steps in our lives.

Church ministries are good and very much needed. However, they don't replace sitting at the feet of Jesus or having daily communication with him. We serve in our church ministries out of love for Jesus, and sitting at his feet will cause us to fall more in love with him. Creating space to hear what Jesus has to say and living out his words in our lives every day will help us to prioritize our church ministries.

Dear Jesus,

I thank you for coming to see me. I love serving your people, but please do not allow me to focus more on church work than on having a relationship with you. Reveal to me the areas of ministry to which you have called me. I want to hear everything you have for me. When you manifest yourself, I don't want to be the one always passing out tissues or giving hugs. I want to be the one lying at the altar, surrendering my will and walking in complete obedience. I love being in your presence.

In Jesus' Name,

Amen

Day 29

Not What I Expected

The year 2009 was a season of "blah" in my life. I was not growing in any area of life except for my stomach and thighs. Lack of focus and vision would be a great way to describe it. Going through the motions and just trying to get through the day was my daily accomplishment. Being a wife, mom, sister, daughter, and friend seemed to consume most of my time. My church attendance was regular, but most of the time, I was not ready to hear from God or even worship him. If Jesus showed up and touched me, it was a blessing but not an expectation. I did what I had always done: sit in the choir stand and shout "Preach, Pastor" at the appropriate time. Then I went home to cook Sunday dinner. I spent a few moments daily in God's Word, but not enough to make a difference in my life. You know, just enough to say that I read my Bible.

Then, I remember praying one day and asking God for help. I was tired and becoming frustrated with the lack of growth in my life. Let me be honest: I didn't know what I was asking God to do with me at that time. I just wanted things to change.

As I look back now, I realize that I could feel God tugging on my heart to read his Word and spend time with him in prayer. So, I would schedule time with him, though sometimes I would fall asleep, watch a movie, or read a book during our scheduled time together. Oh, and I kept asking God to change my situation. I knew that I needed a closer relationship with him, but I didn't know how to get there. Or, let me say that I ignored Jesus, who spoke to my heart and gave me directions on how to draw closer to him.

At the end of the year, I can remember being at church in our annual Watch Night Service on December 31st. This is a tradition in the black church that originated during slavery. It involves asking Jesus to help us again.

Little did I know that God would answer my prayer, but not the way I had anticipated. I had envisioned myself going to church, and then, after an inspirational message, I would go to the altar for prayer. The Holy Spirit would hit me, and I would cry out and fall to the ground, requiring blankets to be placed on my legs and several altar workers to hold me. After about one hour, the saints would get me up and help me to my car because I would still be full of the Spirit and would not be able to walk unassisted. Then, the Lord and I would have this fantastic relationship. I would wake up and desire to read God's Word; he would speak to me, and I would respond in obedience and with enthusiasm.

But God had something else in mind for me. The reality is, after just two months in the new year, God allowed one of the most challenging trials in my life to invade my space.

I can't explain it, but I felt in my heart that something was about to take place. I couldn't put my finger on it. I started praying harder and fasting. One night after church, one of the elders stopped me in the parking lot and said that God had placed me on his heart; he wanted to pray for me. So, he did. I knew then that God was preparing me for something significant, but I had no idea it would be as hard as it was.

Easter that year was the first week in April. One month before Easter, my pastor put the church on a three-week fast every day until 4 pm. I felt compelled to join the fast, so I did. I am so grateful that I obeyed Jesus regarding the fast because, one week after the fast, my world began to unravel. Life as I knew it changed and would never be the same. Everything came crashing down on March 27th at 4:21 pm. I found myself in my closet on the floor, tears streaming down my face, screaming at God and asking why. If you have not questioned God, you are perhaps farther down the road spiritually than I. But I was upset, disappointed, shocked, and scared, all at the same time. I knew that no one but Jesus could help me.

The next year was going to be a spiritual journey or battle like no other. I remember literally crying myself to sleep and waking up with tears. For the next few weeks, I would drop to the side of my bed and ask God why. I then became angry, but I kept praying as much as I could.

After trying to make it on my own, I picked up my Bible (for real this time) and started studying it. Prayer was no longer an option. Speaking to Jesus every day was now a priority. I prayed until my tears stopped. I prayed even though I felt nothing most of the time. I kept praying because I just knew he heard me.

I'm not sure how long it took, but it happened. My heart opened up enough to hear Jesus speaking to me. I heard him through my hurt, and that was when my healing began. I had listened to the voice of Jesus speaking to me before, but this was a new voice, and our relationship began to grow to a different level. As time went on, I stopped asking God why because I knew that there was a purpose for my pain. He was going to use my pain as a platform to minister to others.

Years later, God used my trial to refine my character, and my new character led me back to faith in Him.

So, you see, God answered my prayer—not in the way that I had envisioned, but in a way that a loving, kind father would do for his daughter. When I look back, I see that he walked with me through every step of my trial. I was never alone.

I love the scripture I Peter 5:10, which lets us know that God himself will restore, support, and strengthen us, placing us on a firm foundation after we have suffered a while. God's Word is true. I believe it.

Dear Jesus,

Life seems so hard and unfair right now. I need and want your help. I know that you love me and understand what is best for me. Could you help me to see myself the way you see me? Reveal the purpose of my situation. I want to understand that just because it hurts and I cry doesn't mean that your hand is not at work in my situation. I trust you.

In Jesus' Name,

Amen

Day 30

Seeing the Light

Back in our younger days, my husband and I would fish at night. My husband had the bright idea that fish were more hungry or would bite better at night. One night, we went to our "honey hole," which was our favorite spot to fish. It wasn't as bad as it sounds, as we had a large boat with a small cubby for sleeping and staying warm. While night fishing, if we became tired, we would place bells on our poles, drop the poles in the water, and listen for the bells to ring.

This particular night was like any other night. We arrived on the water in the early evening and got set up for the night.

At about midnight, we noticed the fog rolling in. At first, it was faint, and we could still see several feet around us. However, after a few hours, the fog was weighty, and we could barely see the front of the boat. We decided to get a few hours of sleep, hoping the fog would lift and that we could safely return to the boat dock and go home to get some much-needed rest.

After sleeping several hours, we realized that the fog was staying around longer than anticipated. We discussed our options and decided to try to find our way back to the dock. We had the required lights (green and red) on our boat's front, but it wasn't enough to see clearly in the heavy fog. We had made this trip from our spot to the boat dock at least 50 times. However, that had been during the day, and we could easily see our way. As we slowly moved forward, we came to a point where we could no longer determine our turns on the water. The fog was so thick that I could not see my fingers when I placed my hand out.

Let me admit that I was nervous and praying the entire time. As we kept moving slowly, my husband recognized a small light flashing on the bank. Then he knew it was time to turn left into a slough that would take us to the boat dock. It took us a while, but we made it safely back to the boat dock. I was so thankful for the light that my husband had seen and recognized.

In Psalms 27, David said, "The Lord is my light and my salvation; whom shall I fear? The Lord is the strength of my life, of who shall I be afraid."

If we are not careful and diligent regarding our relationship with Jesus, the spiritual fog will set in while we are sleeping. That season, when we get comfortable, we go a few days without praying or reading God's Word. We become unaware of our surroundings. Then, before we know it, we are surrounded by fog that our enemy brings to distort our vision.

Like my husband and me, you wait to see if it passes. But soon, you realize that your relationship with Jesus is not getting better. You begin to feel an awful sense of disconnection. Then you know that the enemy of your soul has set you up.

You decide to restore your relationship with Jesus. Your first move is to read and study your Bible, as well as to pray daily. I absolutely love Jesus because he adores us and is committed to keeping himself approachable. When we are blindly attempting to make things better, Jesus shines his light so that we can see him. Once we see the light (that never goes out), we can maneuver through the darkest, foggiest situations of our lives.

David clearly understood that the Lord was his light. God was the guiding light in his life. He knew that all he had to do was find and follow the light. If God was leading him, he didn't have to be afraid because he was on the right track.

Suppose you are feeling lost and trying to find your way. Follow Jesus; he is the light for us today. You don't have to be afraid of where he is leading you. He has your best interest at heart.

Dear Jesus,

Thank you for loving me. However, I am lost, or I feel lost. Sometimes I feel like you have abandoned me. You and I have been so close in the past; I want to return to you. I am at a crossroads in my life, and I need your light to shine extra bright so that I can find my way. Please shine so that I don't have to guess whether it's you whom I am following. I know that if I trust you and follow you, I don't have to fear anything.

In Jesus' Name,

Amen

Day 31

He Sees Me

I think everyone wants to be seen. Not my outer appearance; I want others to see my heart. I want others to see my hopes, dreams, desires, hurts, victories, longings, fears, need for touch, and need for a listening ear.

As little girls, we dream of marrying a tall, dark, and handsome man. Those features are useful, but it's not until we are married that we come to understand the things that are important to our marriage. Then, we know and accept the things that our spouses are unable to give us. You know, something only God can provide us with, such as healing, knowing our thoughts, etc. If you don't understand these things, you will have a miserable marriage trying to pull something out of your spouse that he doesn't have. It's draining and frustrating for both you and your spouse.

Real intimacy is when a person sees you—not your failures, body shape, or attitude, but your heart. Sometimes women and men are afraid of intimacy because of what is actually in their hearts. They are fearful of anyone knowing their true desires.

This is why being in a relationship with God is so amazing. Your relationship with God can go as deep as you would like it to be.

I have often read Psalm 139, especially the 14th verse, which says that I am fearfully and wonderfully made. God's Word reminds me that God was intentional when he created me, and I was not a mistake. Ephesians 2:10 says that I am His workmanship created for good works.

One day, I read all of Psalm 139. It begins with "O Lord, thou hast searched me and known me." This lets me know that nothing about me is hidden from God. Nothing I say to him in prayer or mediation will shock him.

The next verse says, "You perceive every movement of my heart and soul, and you understand my every thought before it even enters my mind" (TPT). Now, that is intimacy at its fullest. This is the level of intimacy that we often want to have with others, but it is reserved for God and God alone. Okay, let me keep going before I start to cry. Verses 3 and 4 say, "You are so intimately aware of me, Lord. You read my heart like an open book, and you know all of the words I'm about to speak before I even start a sentence! You know every step I will take before my journey even begins." Let me stop and tell you that my heart is so full right now, thinking about how much God loves me.

As I am writing this book, I have been married for 31 years. My husband is a large man. He stands 6'2" and such-and-such pounds! When he walks into a room, he is noticed immediately. I think it's his size and the attitude that he carries. I can tell you that I always feel protected when I am with him. Like others, our marriage is not perfect, but he is a great protector and provider for our family. He will stop at no lengths to keep us from danger.

There have been seasons of our marriage when I wanted more intimacy from him. This was an extremely frustrating time for me. However, God taught me that he is the one to fulfill my needs and that my husband cannot rise to the level of intimacy that I felt I needed. My husband is a good husband, but he is a horrible God. I had to let God be God in my life. This helped to alleviate frustration in my marriage.

I am sure that you have relationships, whether with your spouse, mother, father, or siblings, that you wish were better. You may feel like you are the only one in the relationship, making an effort to achieve closeness. Let me tell you that people can give only what they have on the inside.

If you are not crying the ugly cry yet, read the 5th verse. It speaks of how God has gone before us, in our future, to prepare the way, and in his amazing kindness, he also follows us. So, he has gone before us and walks behind us as well. That means his love surrounds us. He walks behind us to spare us from the harm of our pasts. In other words, he assures us that our past mistakes won't impact our future.

Lastly, verse 6 says, "This is just too wonderful, deep and incomprehensible! Your understanding of me brings me wonder and strength." I am in total awe of his intimacy, love, peace, and kindness toward me.

The thing is, he knows that we are incapable of returning this level of intimacy to him, but he gives it to us anyway. Listen, he does want your heart.

My challenge for you today is to open your heart to him. You can trust him. Take time to journal or sit and talk to God for a few moments. Share the intimate parts of your heart and soul. Watch your relationship with him change.

Just know that God sees you for who you are, whether in the darkest times or the most joyous moments of your life. God is there and sees you—not just your physical body but also the intricate parts of your heart. He sees, he knows, and he cares.

Jesus,

Your love and concern for me are excellent. I don't understand why you love me so much. Sometimes I feel so unworthy of your love. Could you teach me how to open up more to you? My goal is to trust you with everything important to me. This is scary because I have never had a relationship like this before. I want my relationship with you to grow and grow. I am in this for the long haul.

In Jesus' Name,

Amen

www.ingramcontent.com/pod-product-compliance
Lightning Source LLC
LaVergne TN
LVHW011733060526
838200LV00051B/3165